THE BEST
Aspen
HIKES

ROD MARTINEZ

The Colorado Mountain Club Press
Golden, Colorado

The Best Aspen Hikes
© 2014 by The Colorado Mountain Club

PUBLISHED BY

The Colorado Mountain Club Press
710 Tenth Street, Suite 200, Golden, Colorado 80401
303-996-2743   e-mail: cmcpress@cmc.org

Founded in 1912, The Colorado Mountain Club is the largest outdoor recreation, education, and conservation organization in the Rocky Mountains. Look for our books at your local bookstore or outdoor retailer or online at www.cmc.org/store.

Erika K. Arroyo: design, composition, and production
Eduard B. Avis: copy editor
Christian Green: publisher
Rod Martinez: project manager

CONTACTING THE PUBLISHER
We would appreciate it if readers would alert us to any errors or outdated information by contacting us at the address above.

DISTRIBUTED TO THE BOOK TRADE BY
The Mountaineers Books, 1001 SW Klickitat Way, Suite 201, Seattle, WA 98134, 800-553-4453, www.mountaineersbooks.org

TOPOGRAPHIC MAPS are copyright 2009 and were created using National Geographic TOPO! Outdoor Recreation software (www.natgeomaps.com; 800-962-1643).

COVER PHOTO: The Maroon Bells, from Maroon Lake Trailhead, looking southwest.
Photo by Rod Martinez

We gratefully acknowledge the financial support of the people of Colorado through the Scientific and Cultural Facilities District of greater Denver for our publishing activities.

WARNING: Although there has been an effort to make the trail descriptions in this book as accurate as possible, some discrepancies may exist between the text and the trails in the field. Hiking in mountainous areas—and canyons and deserts as well—is a high-risk activity. This guidebook is not a substitute for your experience and common sense. The users of this guidebook assume full responsibility for their own safety. Weather, terrain conditions, and individual abilities must be considered before undertaking any of the hikes in this guide.

First Edition

ISBN 978-1-937052-08-9

Printed in Korea

This pack guide is dedicated to a great friend, longtime Aspen resident Larry Beidleman, who encouraged me to rediscover the Aspen area for great hikes and photography. But no one other than Larry's son, Neal Beidleman, could better express Larry's love for the Aspen area:

It was the early 1970s and my dad and I were returning from our first multiday overnight hiking/camping trip together. I was maybe 11 years old and was carrying a pack half my weight. My dad wanted to explore a new area to him in the upper Fryingpan. We fished, skipped rocks on flat water till our arms hurt, swatted mosquitos, and my dad told me stories. It was all perfect, even the long walk out in freezing cold, pouring rain. My dad made sure I hopped over the deepest of the puddles, out of principle only, since we were both soaked to the bone in our $5 plastic ponchos and leather clutter shoes. Once back in the old Jeep, I shivered hard until I fell asleep on the drive back to Aspen. Mom made hot chocolate and we both excitedly told her stories of our trip. It couldn't have been better. This was what Aspen and the mountains were all about to my dad and what they came to mean to me.

I would also like to dedicate this pack guide to Larry's best friend and a great friend of mine, Larry's wife, Evelyn. Also to Neal; Neal's wife, Amy; Larry's grandchildren, Reed and Nina; as well as my three granddaughters, Brittany, Nichole, and Samantha. May our young people love the Aspen area like Larry, Neal, Amy, and I do.

And last but not least, I dedicate this pack guide to my best friend and hiking partner, now residing in Minnesota, Jerry Shallman.

Larry And Evelyn Beidleman

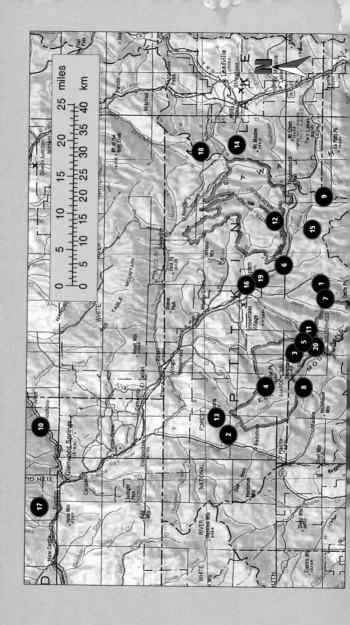

CONTENTS

Looking down valley to Maroon Lake.

PHOTO BY ROD MARTINEZ

THE BEST ASPEN HIKES

FOREWORD

The 20 hiking trails in this pack guide range from one of the most picturesque areas, Maroon Lake, to one of the more remote areas in Colorado, Capitol Lake. You will hike to the top of the highest named pass in Colorado, hike along the base of numerous Fourteeners, and then hike Storm King Mountain Memorial Trail—built in memory of 14 firefighters who died fighting a wildfire in South Canyon, about 10 miles west of Glenwood Springs. Before you tackle the hikes ranked moderate or difficult, I recommend you become acclimated to the altitude.

RATINGS

What distinguishes the difficulty rating of the hikes? Each hiker will see differences in what is termed easy, moderate, and difficult. Among elements in establishing the ratings are:

Elevation gain. A 1,700-foot gain in elevation for a round-trip hike of 3 to 4 miles may be as difficult or as strenuous as one gaining 3,000 feet in a 6- to 8-mile round trip.

Round-trip distance. Normally, an 8- to 10-mile hike is more difficult or strenuous than one of 4 to 6 miles.

Trail characteristics. Is the trail well marked, or do you need to search for continuation of the trail? Are boulder hopping or scree slopes involved? Are there creek/stream crossings, and are they easy or is wading involved? As the difficult elements add up or increase in severity, so will the difficulty rating.

WEATHER

Be aware of and prepared for changes in the weather. If it looks as if it will rain, consider doing the hike another day. An early start will decrease the odds of encountering afternoon thunderstorms. If the weather begins to deteriorate while you are hiking, be cautious and consider turning around.

Once while ascending the Electric Pass Trail, near Aspen, I noticed clouds were beginning to build. After reaching the pass, the clouds were really gathering and the wind began to blow. Instead of relaxing, I quickly turned around and headed back. I talked with other hikers on their way up who seemed unconcerned about the weather, and they did not appear to be carrying any rain gear. About 10:30 AM, I passed more hikers still going up as it began to rain. Shortly thereafter, I cleared the first ridge before the clouds opened up and it began to rain rather hard. I put on my rain jacket and kept going down. In another 0.5 mile, the rain became intense and it started to hail. I finally descended from the last ridge and entered the trees before the storm intensified with flashes of lightning. Because I had the proper equipment and was cautious, I returned safely. Situations such as this are not unusual in the mountains. Don't take chances when the weather is changing.

ROUND-TRIP TIME

The time it takes to complete a hike depends on the physical ability of the hiker and the purpose of the hike. The hikes described in this pack guide might be among the first hikes for some readers, and consequently, it might take them longer to get acclimated to the altitude and tune up muscles little used before. Others might be acclimated and in great shape. The time it takes them to complete these hikes might be considerably shorter.

I happen to be a slow hiker, because I pause frequently to catch my breath and enjoy the scenery. I also stop and take a lot of photographs. I am not a point-and-shoot photographer.

I work at getting the best possible photo (see photography tips on pages 19–20 of this pack guide), so it might take more time to capture the image I am seeking.

The times listed in this pack guide are based on average hikers who want to enjoy their hike. For those who hike for great outdoor exercise, the times probably will be shorter. I recommend you start early to avoid afternoon storms, and begin your return trip in time to make it to the trailhead before it gets dark.

SAFETY

The Ten Essentials Systems, on pages 16–18 of this pack guide, are the Colorado Mountain Club's "systems" to promote safety awareness and give you a list of safety items to carry with you at all times when hiking. Please take the time to read, study, and absorb all the Ten Essentials.

Here are some additional safety measures to consider and make habits:

- Tell someone where you plan to go and when you plan to return. Be specific and stay on the trail. Tell that person to contact authorities in the area you are hiking if he or she does not hear from you by an appointed time.
- Sign in at the trail register. Sign out when you return.
- Consider carrying an emergency locater device. In life-threatening circumstances, it can notify emergency personnel where you are and that you need their help. Keep it readily accessible so you can reach it when necessary. When not hiking, keep it in your vehicle—just in case. There are several available with various features at outdoor equipment retailers.
- Consider purchasing a CORSAR (Colorado Outdoor Recreation Search and Rescue) card. Colorado has a Search and Rescue Fund to help local agencies cover the costs of search-and-rescue operations. Money for the fund is provided by a surcharge on hunting and fishing licenses and vessel, snowmobile, and off-highway vehicle registrations. People who don't have one of those licenses, registrations, or a CORSAR card could be billed for some expenses related to a search and rescue, which can be extensive. A CORSAR card costs $3 annually or $12 for a five-year card. You can purchase a CORSAR card from

outdoor, recreation, and sporting goods retailers and organizations throughout the state. It also can be purchased online; simply search for CORSAR for a link to the state website.

LEAVE NO TRACE

We owe it to present and future generations to care for the wild places. If you pack it in, pack it out—leave only footprints:

- Plan ahead and prepare for the cleanest possible adventure.
- Stay on the trail and don't shortcut on switchbacks; camp on durable surfaces, such as rock or sand. Above timberline, hike on rocks and avoid damaging the tundra. When more than one person is off trail, spread out so you don't start destructive new "social" trails.
- Dispose of all waste properly, including that deposited by your dog. "Pack it in, pack it out."
- Leave what you find—look at it, take a photo, leave it for the next person.
- Minimize campfire impacts—think small and keep the fuel within the fire circle. Unless it is a permanent fire pit, destroy all traces of your fire before leaving your campsite. Forest fires have started from small campfires or their smoldering embers; be extremely cautious in this regard. The best practice is to soak down your fire site.
- Respect wildlife—don't feed them anything and don't intrude on their feeding and breeding areas. Moose deserve your complete respect; they are considered by experts to be the most dangerous animal in the Colorado woods.
- Be considerate of animals and other humans in the woods—don't play your radio or make other unnecessary noise. Part of the lure of the woods is the healing sound of wind through the trees, or the murmur of a stream.

ACKNOWLEDGMENTS

Rarely can you undertake a project that lets you do two things you love—hiking and photography—and then tell about it in a published work. With a little guidance from the Colorado Mountain Club Press editorial staff, I was turned loose to hike and photograph the Aspen area. This project turned out to be a terrific way to spend the summer and early fall. Thanks to Christian Green, who contributed two of the hikes and is publisher of *The Best Aspen Hikes* pack guide.

—ROD MARTINEZ

Wildflowers fill the meadows at the flanks of Grizzly Peak.

PHOTO BY ROD MARTINEZ

Introduction

If you can only visit one part of Colorado for some great hikes, you should choose the Aspen area. Aspen is well known for its skiing, but the hiking trails in this area are second to none. Forty-plus years ago I was introduced to the Aspen area by taking a 10-mile drive from Aspen to Maroon Lake, via Maroon Creek Road. I immediately fell in love with the area. Since then I have made at least three trips annually to Maroon Lake. In late spring the Maroon Bells—North Maroon and Maroon peaks (both Fourteeners)—are still covered in snow; the rivers, creeks, and lakes swell with snowmelt; and numerous waterfalls tumble off the mountainsides. In mid-summer wildflowers abound, but no season is more spectacular or colorful than autumn, when the aspens lining the road to Maroon Lake turn golden and the foliage surrounding the lake morphs into a brilliant display of yellows and oranges. Three trips at different times of the year will give you three different experiences. The Maroon Lake area is typically closed from mid-October to Memorial Day because of snow.

The Aspen area was first populated and used as hunting grounds by the Ute Indians. The Utes began to leave as settlers and miners seeking silver and gold moved in during the 1870s. Aspen was first established as a mining camp in 1879 and a road, of sorts, was built

> **Caveat—on maps and map scales**
>
> In producing this pack guide, we have endeavored to provide the most accurate information possible. This striving for accuracy includes the map segments which follow each trail description. Many of the trails indicated by the red lines, however, include contours, ups and downs, and switchbacks that cannot be depicted on a small map. Thus, with some maps, you may find what looks like a variance between the stated length of the trail and the length of the trail when compared to the scale indicator.
>
> For every trail described in this guide, we list relevant, larger-scale maps of the area you will be hiking in—such as Trails Illustrated and USGS maps. It is always a good practice to secure these larger maps, study them, and understand where the smaller map from the guide fits within the larger map. The best practice is to carry both maps on your hike.

connecting the mining towns of Leadville and Buena Vista to Aspen. This road, Colorado 82, traverses Independence Pass, which is part of one of Colorado's 25 Scenic Byways, the "Top of the Rockies." The pass was also designated by the US Secretary of Transportation as a National Scenic Byway and one of 11 America's Byways designated in Colorado.

Silver was the initial backbone of mining in Aspen, as well as the town of Ashcroft, which is located about 11 miles southwest of Aspen on the Castle Creek Road. Gold was first discovered around the now ghost town of Independence (located three miles west of the top of Independence Pass) on July 4, 1879, hence the town's name. At one point, more than 2,000 people lived in Independence and relied on Aspen and Ashcroft for supplies. Gold prices went bust and so did the mines around Independence in late 1883. Most of the miners then moved to Aspen. Shortly thereafter, the repeal of the Sherman Silver Act of 1893 caused Aspen to "bust." Ashcroft, because of its shallow silver ore deposits, began to lose its 12,000 residents before the bust and declined to the ghost town it is today.

The miners were some of the first people to appreciate nature's beauty in the Aspen area. To really appreciate the beauty of this area one could take a 3- to 5-day backpack hike, a 28-mile loop over four 12,400-foot passes. But there are innumerable day hikes that will get you into four wilderness areas, where you can experience solitude and be surrounded by beauty. There are six Fourteeners—Capitol Peak (14,130 feet), Maroon Peak (14,156 feet), North Maroon Peak (14,014 feet), Castle Peak (14,265 feet), Snowmass Mountain (14,092 feet), and Pyramid Peak (14,018 feet)—located in the immediate area around Aspen. Numerous other 14,000-foot mountains are on the east side of Independence Pass, including the two highest mountains in Colorado, Mount Elbert (14,433 feet) and Mount Massive (14,421 feet), which can be seen from the hikes in the Leadville area. There are numerous other Fourteeners, unofficial Fourteeners (not classified as

Fourteeners for a number of reasons; these include Conundrum Peak [14,060 feet], Massive Green [14,300 feet], and South Elbert [14,134 feet]), as well as numerous Thirteeners, two of the most impressive being Grizzly Peak (13,988 feet) and Cathedral Peak (13,943 feet). However, you do not have to climb any mountain to enjoy the beauty of the Aspen area.

If you climb just one mountain, I recommend the trail to the top of Mount Sopris (twin summits, each 12,953 feet), where you will have great views of Aspen to the south, Glenwood Springs to the north, the Marble area to the west, and as far as the eye can see to the east. With this guide, you can also hike to some of Colorado's most beautiful lakes, including the aforementioned Maroon, American Lake, Crater Lake, Geneva Lake, Grizzly Lake, Native Lake, Timberline Lake, Thomas Lakes, Cathedral Lake, and Capitol Lake, at the base of the impressive and difficult Capitol Peak. The passes in this pack guide—Midway Pass, New York Creek Pass, Buckskin Pass, and the "electrifying" Electric Pass—provide panoramic views that are hard to duplicate unless you are an eagle and can soar over the area. In mid-summer wildflowers can be found in abundance on every hike in this pack guide.

Along the trails of some of the more popular hikes in this pack guide, such as the Maroon Bells Scenic Loop or the Rio Grande Trail in Aspen or Hanging Lake in Glenwood Springs, you may meet people from just about any place in the world. If you wish to enjoy a little more solitude, Avalanche Creek Trail, Midway Pass, New York Creek, or my favorite trail, Difficult Creek, are good choices. Along Difficult Creek Trail, there are places to sit and enjoy the waterfalls as they cascade to the Roaring Fork River, and your only visitor may be an occasional chipmunk or squirrel. Two short but difficult hikes, due to rapid elevation gain, are Ute Trail in Aspen and Hanging Lake in Glenwood Canyon. One of the most poignant trails in all of Colorado is Storm King Mountain Memorial Trail, built by volunteers to commemorate the memory of 14 firefighters

Roaring Fork River parallels Rio Grande Trail for 42 miles to Glenwood Springs.
PHOTO BY ROD MARTINEZ

who lost their lives trying to save the forest from a potentially devastating wildfire directly west of Glenwood Springs.

The hikes in this pack guide cover some of the best trails the Aspen area has to offer, from Leadville to Marble and Glenwood Springs to Aspen. Take time to enjoy the history and abundance of natural beauty in the area, and then come back during different seasons to enjoy a fresh view.

The Ten Essentials Systems

The Colorado Mountain Club (CMC), through CMC Press, is the publisher of this pack guide. For more than 100 years, CMC has fostered safety awareness and safe practices in the wilderness, and has distilled the essential safety items down to a list known as "The Ten Essentials." We present it here in a "systems" approach. Carrying the items from this list that are appropriate for the location, mileage, and elevation of your hike will help you be fully prepared for every trip and able to survive the unexpected emergency. We encourage all hikers to study, adopt, and teach The Ten Essentials Systems as part of their own outdoors regimen.

1. **Hydration.** Carry at least 2 liters or quarts of water on any hike. For arid country or desert hiking, carry more. Keep an extra water container in your vehicle and hydrate both before and after your hike. Don't wait until you are thirsty—stay hydrated.

2. **Nutrition.** Eat a good breakfast before your hike; pack a full and healthy lunch, including fruits, vegetables, and carbohydrates. Carry healthy snacks such as trail mix and nutrition bars.

3. **Sun protection.** Start with sunscreen with an SPF rating of at least 45 and reapply it as you hike. Wear sunglasses and a wide-brimmed hat, and use lip balm. These protections are important anywhere in Colorado, especially at high elevations and in desert areas.

4. **Insulation.** Be aware that weather in Colorado can go through extreme changes in a very short time. Think warm and think dry—even in arid areas. Dress with wool or synthetic inner and outer layers. Cotton retains moisture and does not insulate well; it should

not be part of your hiking gear. Carry a warm hat, gloves, and extra socks. Always include a rain/wind parka and rain pants—on you or in your pack. Extra clothing weighs little and is a great safety component.

5. **Navigation.** You should attain at least minimal proficiency with a map and compass. A GPS unit can add to your ability, but it's not a substitute for the two basics. Before a hike, study your route, and the surrounding country, on a good map of the area. Refer to the map as needed on the trail.

6. **Illumination.** Include a headlamp or flashlight in your gear, preferably both. With a headlamp, your hands are kept free. Avoid hiking in the dark if at all possible.

7. **First Aid.** Buy or assemble an adequate first-aid kit. Some items to include:
   - Ace bandages; a bandana, which can double as a sling.
   - Duct tape—good for a bandage, blister protection, or rips in your clothes.
   - A small bottle of alcohol or hydrogen peroxide for cleaning a wound.
   - Latex gloves.
   - Specific medications for you and your companions.
   - Toilet paper and Ziploc bags for carrying it out.

Note: This is not a comprehensive list—tailor it and add items for your own perceived needs and intended activities.

8. **Fire.** The best practice is to avoid open fires except in emergency situations. For when you may need to build a fire, carry waterproof matches in a watertight container, a lighter, or a commercial fire starter such as a fire ribbon. Keep these items dry and ensure that all of them will work in cold or wet weather. If needed, tree sap or dry pine needles can help start a fire.

Early morning sun peeking through stately aspens.

9. **Repair kit and emergency tools.** A pocketknife or multitool and duct tape or electrician's tape are good for various repairs. For emergencies, carry a whistle and signal mirror.

10. **Emergency shelter.** Carry a space blanket and nylon cord or a bivouac sack. Large plastic leaf bags are handy for temporary rain gear, pack covers, or survival shelters. On your way out, use this for trash left by careless hikers.

Photography Tips

We see many beautiful subjects in the outdoors that we would like to remember. Here are a few tips to help you take great photographs and enjoy, time and again, the places where you've been:

- Don't forget to take your camera with you. As you hike, keep it within easy reach.
- Carry extra memory cards so you can take enough photographs to properly record your hike and what you saw.
- Charge your batteries before leaving and take extras if you will be out more than one day.
- Before leaving home, set your camera's resolution to the highest setting possible. Check your manual to see how to do this. Another name for resolution is image quality. You want to use every pixel that you paid for when you bought your camera. A higher setting will give you the ability to capture the light and dark tones as well as all the colors your eyes can see.
- Be prepared. Most hikes start early in the morning, so have your camera out and be prepared to capture the early-morning light on the mountains or animals moving around.
- Hold your camera steady. The closer the camera is to your face, the steadier it will be. Your photo should not have that unsteady, out-of-focus look.
- Place your whole subject in the frame, and fill the frame with your subject. If you are taking photos of the mountains, be sure to include the tops. Zoom in to crop out those items that do not add to the photo. I recommend vertical photos as opposed to horizontal ones when you are taking photos of trees, flowers, people, and other vertical objects.

13,988-foot Grizzly Peak to the southwest of Midway Trail.

PHOTO BY ROD MARTINEZ

The vertical format allows you to increase the size of your subject as you zoom in.

- The best way to learn is from your mistakes. Take lots of photos, trying different angles and settings. Try photographing the same images twice, once with a horizontal orientation and once vertical. Remember, a memory card can be reused, and those pixels are free.
- If all else fails, read the manual.

WILDLIFE VIEWING TIPS

Fade into the woodwork (or woods): Wear natural colors and unscented lotions, if any. Be as quiet as possible—walk softly, move slowly.

Keep to the sidelines: Watch animals from a distance they consider safe. Use binoculars or a telephoto lens to get a closer view. Stay away from nests.

Timberline Lake.

PHOTO BY CHRISTIAN GREEN

Use your senses
- **Eyes:** Look up, down, and all around for animal or bird signs such as scat, nests, or tracks. Learn to distinguish these wildlife signatures.
- **Ears:** Listen for animal sounds or movement.
- **Nose:** Be alert to musky scents or strange odors.

Think like an animal: When will an animal eat, nap, drink, bathe?

Optimize your watching: The ultimate wildlife-watching experience is of behaviors—viewing animals without interrupting their normal activities. As a rule, dusk and dawn are the best times for this rewarding experience.

—*Rod Martinez*

1. American Lake Trail

BY ROD MARTINEZ

MAPS	Trails Illustrated, Independence Pass, Number 127; USGS, Hayden Peak 7.5 minute
ELEVATION GAIN	1,970 feet
RATING	Moderate–difficult
ROUND-TRIP DISTANCE	6.5 miles
ROUND-TRIP TIME	5–6 hours
NEAREST LANDMARK	Ashcroft

COMMENT: American Lake resides almost 2,000 feet above Castle Creek Valley, which is the very scenic valley directly southeast of Maroon Creek Valley. The wide valley is equally as beautiful as the more popular Maroon Creek Valley, especially during the fall when the aspen leaves are turning from green to gold. A little more than 1.0 mile from the American Lake Trailhead is the ghost town site of Ashcroft, which is on the National Register of Historic Places. Twelve of the original 15 buildings are still standing. Take the time after your hike to relive the history of the area. Farther up the dirt road is the trailhead to Cathedral Lake and Electric Pass. (Electric Pass, a challenging hike, is described in this pack guide on pages 46–49). The trailhead to 14,265-foot Castle Peak is farther down Castle Creek Valley Road—the 2-wheel-drive trailhead is 2.0 miles and the 4-wheel-drive trailhead is 3.0 miles. You can also climb another unofficial Fourteener, Conundrum Peak, at 14,064 feet, during the climb of Castle Peak. Castle Peak is the highest mountain in the Elk Range and the twelfth highest in Colorado. Conundrum Peak is not officially recognized as a Fourteener, because it does not rise 300 feet above the connecting saddle with Castle Peak. American Lake may be less popular than nearby Cathedral Lake and not as difficult as the nearby Fourteeners, but this

Scree slopes of the surrounding 12,000- and 13,000-foot peaks.

PHOTO BY ROD MARTINEZ

hike is well worth the effort. It is steep and challenging, but you are rewarded with a beautiful alpine lake in a majestic setting of 12,000- and 13,000-foot peaks. This pristine lake, which is fed mainly by snowmelt and rainfall, sits in a bowl surrounded by scree slopes and the aforementioned peaks.

GETTING THERE: From downtown Aspen travel 0.5 mile west to the roundabout and take a right on Castle Creek Road. After 10.0 miles you will arrive at the Elk Mountain Lodge on your left. On your right will be a large parking lot and the trailhead for American Lake.

THE ROUTE: The trail leaves the parking lot with a slight jog to the north as it climbs steeply along a wooded gulch and through aspens. The trail merges with an old road and in a few yards crosses a stream that flows under the road. In about another 200 yards take the fork in the trail that goes to the left. After a 0.25-mile hike through the aspens, you will take a right and begin ascending again at a steady but moderate climb up three switchbacks. One side of the valley is forested in the deep green of conifers and the area through which you are hiking is covered in aspens. This makes for a very colorful hike in the fall. At the 1.0-mile mark you will begin a traverse that takes a dip after 0.5

Looking up the Crystal Valley toward Castle Peak. PHOTO BY ROD MARTINEZ

mile, where you will enter an evergreen forest. The grade becomes more gradual as you hike along the edge of large grassy slopes. About 100 yards before reentering the woods you will see a sign pointing out the hard-to-see Sandy Range Trail. Stay on the level as you go through the forest for a short distance before you climb to the crest of the ridge at 2.2 miles. Take the curve to the right and continue to ascend and traverse the south side of the ridge as you begin to view the southern end of Castle Creek Valley. The higher you go the more the view opens and the aspen groves unfold below you. During the fall this is one of those photo opportunities you will not forget. Again you will leave the aspens and after 0.1 mile reenter the coniferous woods. About 2.7 miles from the trailhead you will enter an open alpine setting, with rocky slopes, fantastic wildflowers (from mid-July to mid-August), and a few scattered trees. Next you

will come to a slope slightly above the lake. Walk the few final yards to the shore and photograph the marvelous reflections of American Lake. Retrace your steps back to the trailhead.

A simple golden leaf.

PHOTO BY ROD MARTINEZ

2. Avalanche Creek Trail

BY ROD MARTINEZ

MAPS	Trails Illustrated, Maroon Bells/Redstone/Marble, Number 128; USGS, Redstone 7.5 minute
ELEVATION GAIN	960 feet
RATING	Moderate
ROUND-TRIP DISTANCE	5.4 miles
ROUND-TRIP TIME	3 hours
NEAREST LANDMARK	Avalanche Campground

COMMENT: Avalanche Creek Trail can take you to myriad other trails located in the western end and less visited part of the Maroon Bells-Snowmass Wilderness Area. To reach the trailhead you will go through Basalt and Carbondale and drive close to the unique town of Redstone, home of the historic Redstone Castle. The Avalanche Creek Trail intersects with Hell Roaring, East Creek, West Fork, and Capitol Creek trails, all of which lead you to the heart of the Maroon Bells-Snowmass Wilderness Area. This trail, which is also used by backpackers and horseback riders, is a great 5.4-mile round-trip hike. Avalanche Lake is 22.0 miles round trip from the trailhead, which can make for a fun backpacking hike.

As soon as you turn off Colorado 133 onto Forest Road 310 you will be entering a Rocky Mountain bighorn sheep management area and seasonal closure area. This road is closed to all vehicle traffic from November 30 to May 1. If you choose to do this hike during that timeframe, you will need to park right after you turn onto FR 310 and hike an additional 2.5 miles to the trailhead.

GETTING THERE: From Aspen drive 32 miles west on Colorado 82, then turn left at CO 133 and continue south 12.5 miles.

The trail winds its way through tall ferns.   PHOTO BY ROD MARTINEZ

Turn left at the sign for Avalanche Creek and follow the road (FR 310) for 2.5 miles to Avalanche Campground and to the parking area at the southeast end of the campground.

THE ROUTE: There is no sign to identify the trailhead, but the trail is obvious and about 50 yards to the left of Bulldog Creek. A few yards into the trail you will come to an intersection. Stay to the left; the right fork will take you to the creek. A few yards farther down the trail there is a sign indicating you are on Trail #1959, Avalanche Creek Trail. As you begin to ascend into the aspen and coniferous forest, you will enter the Maroon Bells-Snowmass Wilderness Area, 0.25 mile from the trailhead. For the first 2.0 miles of the hike, the trail is relatively level as you go in and out of the forest. Avalanche Creek will be on your right and you will be able to catch glimpses of the creek and its cascades and waterfalls as it continues to flow approximately 2.0 miles to Crystal River.

At 1.25 miles from the trailhead you will come to a small creek that could be difficult to cross when the water flow is higher, such as after a snowmelt. There are rocks in the creek, along with some logs, but the logs are not sturdy enough to provide sound footing, so use the rocks where possible. After another 1.0 mile, you will come to a second creek that has

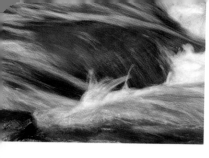

Avalanche Creek rushes downward to the Crystal River.

PHOTO BY ROD MARTINEZ

larger rocks to help you cross. A few yards past the second creek you will enter a large meadow filled with ferns and wildflowers during the summer. You will now begin to ascend as you move away from Avalanche Creek and enter a lengthy grove of tall stately aspens. At 2.5 miles from the trailhead you will leave the aspens. Here, the roar of Hell Roaring Creek grabs your attention as it dramatically falls to Avalanche Creek. At the intersection with Hell Roaring Trail, continue straight past the sign for Hell Roaring Trail (#1960), and you will descend 0.2 mile to a bridge to cross Hell Roaring Creek. This is

the turnaround point for this hike. Retrace your steps back to the intersection with Trail #1960 (Hell Roaring Trail), where you can continue to the Avalanche Creek Trailhead or take a side trip up the canyon on Trail #1960 for 0.5 to 1.0 mile to get great views of Hell Roaring Creek canyon.

Working away at an abundance of flora.

PHOTO BY ROD MARTINEZ

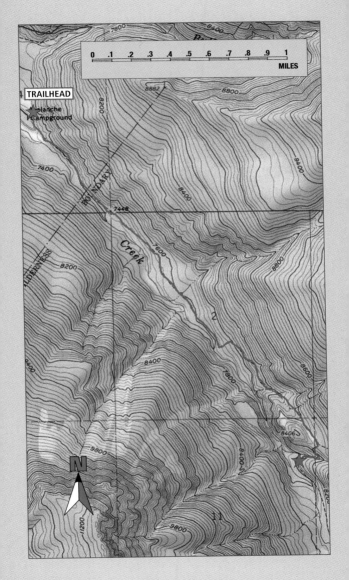

3. Buckskin Pass Trail

BY ROD MARTINEZ

MAPS	Trails Illustrated, Maroon Bells/ Redstone/Marble, Number 128; USGS, Maroon Bells 7.5 minute
ELEVATION GAIN	2,882 feet
RATING	Difficult–strenuous
ROUND-TRIP DISTANCE	9.6 miles
ROUND-TRIP TIME	8–10 hours
NEAREST LANDMARK	Maroon Lake

COMMENT: At 12,462 feet, Buckskin Pass is one of four passes backpackers cross as they hike the 26-mile loop trail from Maroon Lake. In addition to Buckskin Pass, you go over Trail Rider Pass (12,420 feet), Frigid Air Pass (12,415 feet), and West Maroon Pass (12,500 feet) on your way back to Maroon Lake. Whichever way you hike, the trip is stunning and the views are spectacular.

When you leave Crater Lake the trail ascends toward Buckskin Pass as it skirts alongside the impressive North Maroon Peak and follows the base of the Sleeping Sexton, a 13,460-foot mountain that is photographed about as often as the famous Maroon Bells, because it's right next to North Maroon Peak. As you ascend farther look to the southeast and enjoy some of your first views of 14,018-foot Pyramid Peak. The farther you ascend to Buckskin Pass, the better the views of North Maroon Peak and Pyramid Peak, because they become more impressive as they separate from the mountain ridges and lower peaks that block your view at lower elevations. As you continue ascending farther into Minnehaha Gulch, you will be amazed at the amount and variety of wildflowers in mid-to late summer; it feels as if they will never end and they don't, even at the top of Buckskin Pass.

13,460-foot Sleeping Sexton sits 0.5 mile north of North Maroon Peak.

PHOTO BY ROD MARTINEZ

GETTING THERE: From downtown Aspen travel 0.5 mile to the roundabout and take a right (west) on Maroon Creek Road. Arrive at the ranger station at 5.0 miles. At 9.5 miles the road ends at the very large day-use parking lot. Please read the vehicle restrictions and fees that are described in the Maroon Bells Scenic Loop on pages 62–65 of this pack guide.

THE ROUTE: The trail, Maroon-Snowmass #1975, begins at the west end of the parking lot. To the right of the US Forest Service bulletin board, 0.5 mile from the Maroon Lake Scenic Trailhead at the end of Maroon Lake, look for a small sign to Crater Lake. For further description of the hike to Crater Lake, please read the trail route as described in this pack guide on pages 38–41. At 1.7 miles from the Crater Lake Trail sign, you will emerge into a short grassy meadow at the edge of Crater Lake. The trail separates, with the right-hand fork of the Maroon-Snowmass Trail (#1975) continuing on to Buckskin Pass, this hike's destination.

The trail begins to ascend steeply through aspens and conifers, and at 2.4 miles from the Crater Lake Trailhead you will enter Minnehaha Gulch. As you continue to ascend through the thinning trees, stop to admire and photograph

14,018-foot Pyramid Peak is 2.0 miles east of the "Bells", as it guards West Maroon Valley.

North Maroon Peak, the Sleeping Sexton, and Pyramid Peak, which is behind you. At 2.9 miles you will cross a stream with nice cascades as it tumbles to Crater Lake. (In early spring, snowmelt and runoff make most streams larger and a little more difficult to cross.) As the trail continues, you will travel through meadows of wildflowers and pass downed trees caused by avalanches that descended from the surrounding mountains and passes.

At 3.4 miles the trail reaches the end of Minnehaha Gulch and then climbs another steep gully filled with wildflowers. It then emerges into a beautiful basin. Looking straight ahead Buckskin Pass appears on your left and Willow Pass is slightly hidden on your right. The trail junction of Buckskin Pass and Willow Pass is 3.8 miles from the trailhead. Willow Pass is reached via Willow Lake Trail (#1978). Continue on Maroon-Snowmass Trail (#1975) as it zigzags its way up the final 0.8 mile and almost 500 feet in elevation to Buckskin Pass, where you will find spectacular panoramic views of Snowmass Peak (13,620 feet), Hagerman Peak (13,841 feet), and Snowmass Mountain (14,092 feet), and the stunning Snowmass Lake to the west. Capitol Peak (14,130 feet) and Mount Daly (13,300 feet) are to the northwest and Pyramid Peak dominates the skyline to the east. Be aware of storms; it began to hail when I topped the pass. Retrace your steps back to the trailhead.

4. Capitol Creek Trail

BY ROD MARTINEZ

MAPS	Trails Illustrated, Carbondale/ Basalt, Number 143 and Maroon Bells/Redstone/Marble, Number 128; USGS, Capitol Peak 7.5 minute
ELEVATION GAIN	2,200 feet (600 feet lost and then regained)
RATING	Difficult
ROUND-TRIP DISTANCE	11–13 miles
ROUND-TRIP TIME	10–12 hours
NEAREST LANDMARK	Basalt

COMMENT: At 14,130 feet, Capitol Peak, which earned its name because it resembles the US Capitol, dominates the view along most of the 11 miles to the edge of Capitol Lake, or 13.0 miles to the base of Capitol Peak. At the base of Capitol Peak, Capitol Lake is a starkly beautiful jade-green lake that is devoid of the meadows of grass and/or wildflowers that surround most mountain lakes. This lake is encircled by a colossal jumble of boulders that at one time were part of the surrounding massif of Capitol Peak, which towers more than 1,800 feet above the south end of the lake. Climbers set up base camp close to the lake so they can spend the next day conquering one of the most challenging climbs of Capitol Peak—from 13,300-foot Mount Daly, to a 13,664-foot subpeak of Capitol Peak named K-2, and then from K-2 to the summit of Capitol Peak, where one must traverse a very narrow 100-foot section called the "Knife Edge." As you enjoy Capitol Lake take the time to look at the "Knife Edge" from below and see if you can spot, either by using binoculars or a telephoto camera lens, climbers along this edge. It is a sight you may never forget as they straddle their way to the top.

Capitol Lake guards 14,130-foot Capitol Peak, one of the most difficult Fourteeners to climb.

PHOTO BY ROD MARTINEZ

From the west side of Capitol Lake you can hike another 1.0 mile to 12,060-foot Capitol Pass and the Avalanche Creek Trail. This is a long and difficult day hike because of the distance, but it can certainly be done on longer summer days. I backpack to campsites near the lake so that I can enjoy the lake, Capitol Pass, and the awesome beauty of Mount Daly and Capitol Peak.

GETTING THERE: From the roundabout in Aspen drive 14 miles west on Colorado 82 and turn left on Old Snowmass Road. Continue 1.8 miles to a "T" intersection, turn right and go 4.9 miles until the pavement ends. Even though there is a dead-end sign here, continue left on the dirt road until you see a trailhead parking area at 8.1 miles. You can hike in from here or farther up the road, but after 9.3 miles the road does get rougher and 4-wheel drive is recommended for the last 0.9 mile to the trailhead on your left.

THE ROUTE: From the trailhead, the trail immediately begins to drop over the ridge and descend 600 feet in the first 0.5 mile. Once at the base of the ridge you will go over an irrigation ditch, through a large meadow, and then to the only bridge spanning Capitol Creek. At 1.0 mile, the trail intersects with the Nelson Creek Trail, which heads east. At 2.0 miles, you

Aspen groves lead you to Capitol Lake and Peak.

PHOTO BY ROD MARTINEZ

will pass through a large meadow where you will have even better views of your destination. At about 3.0 miles the trail will curve west to avoid a ridge. The trail goes through a tall stand of willows, from where it then ascends into another large meadow. The trail then reenters the trees and intersects with the Capitol Ditch Trail, 3.3 miles from the trailhead. At 3.8 miles from the trailhead, the trail intersects with the West Snowmass Trail.

Approximately 0.5 mile from this intersection you will pass through a wooden fence and gate that marks the boundary for a grazing allotment. Once you pass through the gate, close it after you. Within 1.0 mile the trail switchbacks steeply up a headwall, and then crosses Capitol Creek over a sturdy log. In 0.25 mile the trail crosses back over the stream and through meadows of wildflowers. Between 5.7 and 6.0 miles from the trailhead, there are a few great camping spots. As you reach the lake, trails lead in different directions; for example, to the peak on the left or to Capitol Pass on your right. Stop and enjoy the lake, the peaks, and what you have accomplished. Retrace your steps back to the final steep 600-foot ascent to the trailhead.

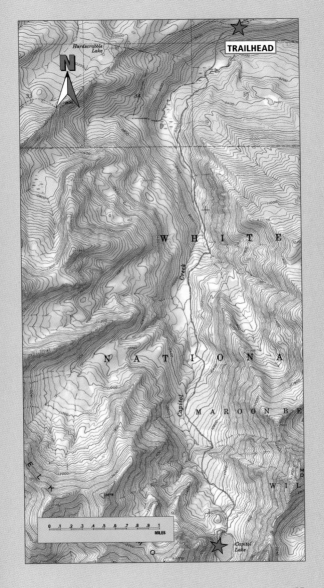

N

Hardscrabble
Lake

33

34

35

W   H   I   T   E

Creek

N   A   T   I   O   N   A

Capitol

M A R O O N   BE

ELK

WIL

0 1 2 3 4 5 6 7 8 9 1
MILES

Capitol
Lake

CAPITOL CREEK TRAIL

5. Crater Lake Trail

BY ROD MARTINEZ

MAPS	Trails Illustrated, Maroon Bells/ Redstone/Marble, Number 128; USGS, Maroon Bells 7.5 minute
ELEVATION GAIN	500 feet
RATING	Moderate
ROUND-TRIP DISTANCE	3.6 miles
ROUND-TRIP TIME	3–4 hours
NEAREST LANDMARK	Maroon Lake

COMMENT: At the end of the Maroon Creek Valley sits the Fourteeners North Maroon Peak (14,014 feet), Maroon Peak (14,156 feet), and Pyramid Peak (14,018 feet), as well as a couple of Thirteeners, Sleeping Sexton (at 13,460, this is the high point of the ridge between Buckskin Pass and the Maroon Bells) and Thunder Pyramid (a 13,932-foot summit, 0.7 mile south of Pyramid Peak). These mountains, which surround Crater Lake, are composed of conspicuously layered late Paleozoic sedimentary rock. They are often photographed for the maroon color and its contrast with the blue sky and the colorful aspens, whether they are green or gold. Please take the time to read the Forest Service bulletin board, located at the end of Maroon Lake, which discusses "The Deadly Bells" and explains that you will be entering the Maroon Bells-Snowmass Wilderness Area. The area covers 181,117 acres and is one of the five original Colorado wilderness areas designated in 1964. It was enlarged in 1980 to become Colorado's fourth-largest wilderness area. Also, read and understand the wilderness regulations so you can help maintain this beautiful, yet heavily used, pristine area in central Colorado. West Maroon Creek fills crystal clear Crater Lake, which lies in the basin between the Maroon

Crater Lake at the base of the Maroon Bells.   PHOTO BY ROD MARTINEZ

Bells, Pyramid Peak, West Maroon Pass, and the rockslide on the east end that helped create this picturesque area.

GETTING THERE: From downtown Aspen travel 0.5 mile to the roundabout and take a right (west) on Maroon Creek Road. At 3.5 miles you will pass through the T-Lazy-7 Ranch before arriving at the ranger station at 5.0 miles. At 9.5 miles the road ends at the very large but restricted day-use parking lot and restroom facilities. Please read the vehicle restrictions and fees that are described in the Maroon Bells Scenic Loop Trail in this pack guide.

THE ROUTE: The trail begins at the west end of the parking lot just past the restrooms. For 0.5 mile follow the easy and wide path along the north side of Maroon Lake. To the right of the Forest Service bulletin board look for a smaller sign pointing to Crater Lake. This is the trailhead for this hike. The trail enters a thick aspen forest and Maroon Creek is to your left as you begin your ascent. The hike is steep in some places for the first 1.0 mile, but generally it is a moderate ascent. The trail is rocky and dry, especially when you are hiking through the treeless scree slopes and boulder fields formed by rockfalls years ago. One of these rock slides dammed the valley and created Crater Lake, which is filled

Maroon Creek cascades down to Maroon Lake.

by Maroon Creek. Be careful and aware of the rocks that are underfoot, because they may be loose and uneven, which is why good sturdy, rugged hiking boots are recommended on this and many other hikes. As you go through the aspen forest mixed with fir and spruce, you will get occasional glimpses of the surrounding mountains and West Maroon Creek, which is fast flowing, especially in the spring, creating cascades, small waterfalls, and pools as it races downhill to reach Maroon Lake. After hiking through the large boulder field, 1.7 miles from the trailhead, you will emerge into a short grassy meadow, which is the edge of Crater Lake. This point provides spectacular scenery, because the lake is in the basin surrounded by the aforementioned Fourteeners and Thirteeners. The trail separates at the beginning of the lake, with the right-hand side going to Buckskin Pass and Willow Pass. The main trail, on the left side, continues on for about 5.0 miles, via a long climb at the far end to 12,500-foot West Maroon Pass. Hike the main trail alongside the lake for about 0.33 mile until you reach the southern end of Crater Lake, where Pyramid Peak reveals its beauty. Take a break and enjoy the scenery before retracing your steps.

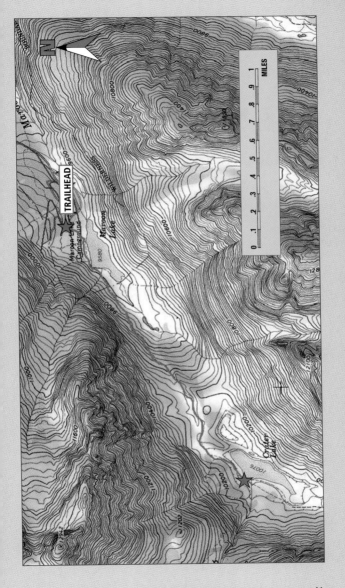

6. Difficult Creek Trail

BY ROD MARTINEZ

MAPS	Trails Illustrated, Aspen/ Independence Pass, Number 127; USGS, Independence Pass 7.5 minute
ELEVATION GAIN	1,340 feet
RATING	Easy–moderate
ROUND-TRIP DISTANCE	6.0 miles
ROUND-TRIP TIME	3–4 hours
NEAREST LANDMARK	Aspen

COMMENT: I could not find a description of why this creek and trail are called Difficult. Perusing the dictionary I found these definitions for the word difficult: Hard to do or accomplish; demanding considerable effort or skill; arduous; hard to endure; trying; hard to please, satisfy. This trail fits none of these descriptions. It is easy to moderate, with a modest elevation gain. It is a very enjoyable day hike, as you ascend through a forest of aspens and varying conifers. In places throughout the trail, wild berries grow thick along its edges and wildflowers are sprinkled along the forest floor. The trailhead is located on the edge of Difficult Campground and only 4.0 miles from downtown Aspen, but I did not encounter any other hikers until I was almost all the way back to the trailhead. For nearly three hours I enjoyed the solitude of the area and the sounds of birds, squirrels, and chipmunks as they went about their business. The hike is not arduous, even though there are some steep stretches along the trail. The most difficult part of the hike was when I finally decided to turn around and head back after I had enjoyed the sights and sounds of Difficult Creek at the end of the trail. The creek cascades

Difficult Creek flows to the Roaring Fork River.   PHOTO BY ROD MARTINEZ

down the mountainside for almost 0.25 mile as you hike alongside it. I was very pleased with this hike; it provided two things I enjoy in a hike: solitude and the ability to connect with nature.

GETTING THERE: From downtown Aspen travel east 4.7 miles on Colorado 82 to the turnoff on your right to Difficult Campground. Go 0.6 mile until you see Difficult Campground. Park in a large area just to the right of the campground entrance.

THE ROUTE: The trailhead is located on the southeast corner of the parking area. Follow the group camping trail for about 100 feet to where it crosses a dirt road that leads to some outdoor restrooms and the group camping site. Stay straight and you will see the sign for Difficult Trail. In a few yards you will cross an area that may have high water in late spring from snowmelt and runoff flowing to the Roaring Fork River. A few more feet after this you will cross a bridge that fords the Roaring Fork River. The trail then ascends the bank of the Roaring Fork River and passes

A nice level part of the trail through pine trees.

PHOTO BY ROD MARTINEZ

through a broad sagebrush area, eventually reaching Difficult Creek in about 0.5 mile. In another 0.1 mile you will enter the 166,938-acre Collegiate Peaks Wilderness Area. The first steep ascent is about 0.25 mile; then it levels off as you go through another stretch of trees for an additional 0.25 mile. After another ascent the trail once again levels off for a long stretch, about 0.4 mile, as you travel alongside a number of downed trees. For the next 0.5 mile you go through more forests of tall and stately aspens, then after a short ascent enter a stand of tall conifers. In a few yards the trail takes a sweeping right turn and continues upward for about 0.5 mile to a large boulder field full of rocks covered by colorful yellow lichen. A few hundred yards farther up the trail you will begin to once again hear Difficult Creek. In another 0.1 mile you will turn left and the creek will be right in front of you. Follow it uphill as you admire the many cascades and waterfalls—it is a sight to see. In another 0.25 mile the trail goes by some old cabins and then begins to fade and get lost in the rocks of

another large boulder field. Turn around here and once again enjoy the forest as you retrace your steps to the trailhead.

An old but sturdy bridge crosses Difficult Creek at the trailhead.

PHOTO BY ROD MARTINEZ

THE BEST ASPEN HIKES

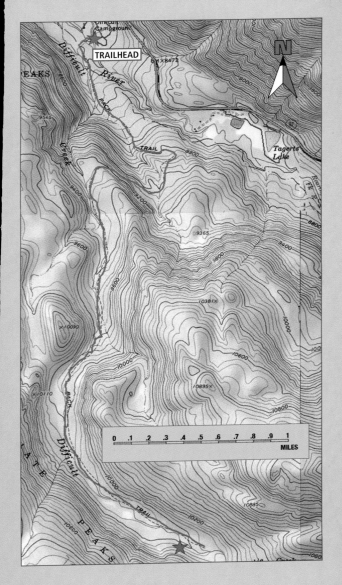

7. Electric Pass Trail

BY ROD MARTINEZ

MAPS	Trails Illustrated, Aspen/ Independence Pass, Number 127; USGS, Hayden Peak 7.5 minute
ELEVATION GAIN	3,620 feet
RATING	Difficult–strenuous
ROUND-TRIP DISTANCE	11 miles
ROUND-TRIP TIME	8–10 hours
NEAREST LANDMARK	Ghost town of Ashcroft

COMMENT: If you are looking for a challenge and desire to experience beautiful one-of-a-kind scenery, this is the hike for you. This trail is difficult to strenuous because of the 3,620 feet in elevation gain. The trail ends at 13,500 feet, at Electric Pass, which is only 500 feet short of the lowest Fourteeners and only 135 feet from the summit of Electric Pass Peak. This may be your opportunity to "bag" a Thirteener. From the pass, which is Colorado's highest named pass, the panoramic views are some of the most spectacular in Colorado. Six of Colorado's Fourteeners—Capitol Peak (14,130 feet), North Maroon (14,014 feet) and Maroon (14,156 feet) peaks, Snowmass Mountain (14,092 feet), Pyramid Peak (14,018 feet), and Castle Peak (14,265 feet), as well as numerous Thirteeners, including the rugged 13,943-foot volcanic extrusion Cathedral Peak, and the unofficial Fourteener Conundrum Peak (14,060 feet)—can be seen from the pass. Anywhere you look the view is spectacular, but beware of approaching storm clouds. If storm clouds gather, retrace your steps back to the trailhead so you will not experience how Electric Pass got its name, from the static electricity that many feel as storms approach. Potentially high winds and chilly temperatures are additional storm hazards.

The trail continues upward to Electric Pass and Peak on the right.

PHOTO BY ROD MARTINEZ

GETTING THERE: From the roundabout, 0.5 mile west of Aspen, travel an additional 10.6 miles on Castle Creek Road to Ashcroft. One mile after Ashcroft continue to the right and travel an additional 0.7 mile to the large parking lot by the trailhead.

THE ROUTE: This trail takes you to Cathedral Lake, as well as to Electric Pass and Electric Pass Peak. The majority of hikers opt only to go to Cathedral Lake. From the trailhead, the trail ascends slowly through an aspen grove and stays parallel to Castle Creek Road for the first 0.5 mile, at which point you will reach Pine Creek. The trail turns to the right and for the next 1.1 miles you will climb in a westerly direction as you gain 1,000 feet in elevation. The trail is close enough to Pine Creek that you can hear the rushing water, but not so close that you need to cross it. In another 0.3 mile, or 1.4 miles from the trailhead, you will enter a beautiful basin where the trail levels for a short distance. As you leave the basin and the large boulder and scree field, you will ascend a steep set of switchbacks that climb 200 feet in a little less than 0.5 mile to a higher cirque where Cathedral Lake is located. About 0.25 mile from the top you will see the trail leading to the left that will take you to Cathedral Lake. It is at this junction where the trail to the

13,943-foot Cathedral Peak is one of Colorado's top 100 peaks.

left (Cathedral Lake Trail #984) will take you to Cathedral Lake. Take the trail to the right, which is now Electric Pass Trail, to continue to Electric Pass.

The trail is now halfway to the top of Electric Pass. There are three different side trails on the left that will take you to Cathedral Lake. Follow the trail on the right each time to continue to your destination. Cathedral Peak's 13,943-foot East Ridge, with its jagged spires, makes for a picturesque backdrop as you wind your way through the willows and gorgeous fields of wildflowers. At 1.7 miles from the first intersection with the trail to Cathedral Lake, you will reach the saddle for Leahy Peak. At the saddle turn left and follow the more obscure trail as it traverses a talus slope westward. Be cautious of footing as you switchback your way through the rocks to the top of Electric Pass. This last 0.5 mile, which is steep and very rocky, may be the most dangerous part of the trail, but the reward at the top of the pass is unsurpassed. Sit and enjoy the views on all sides before retracing your steps back to the trailhead, unless

you wish to take one of the side trails for 0.3 mile one way to Cathedral Lake or follow the ridge to the top of Electric Pass Peak.

Cathedral Lake is at the base of Cathedral Peak.

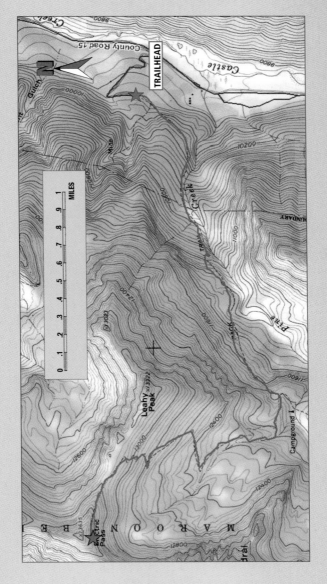

eneva Lake Trail

BY ROD MARTINEZ

	Trails Illustrated, Maroon Bells/ Redstone/Marble, Number 128; USGS, Snowmass Mountain and Marble 7.5 minute
ELEVATION GAIN	1,200 feet
RATING	Moderate
ROUND-TRIP DISTANCE	4.0 miles
ROUND-TRIP TIME	3–4 hours
NEAREST LANDMARK	Marble

COMMENT: The hardest part of this trail is getting to the trailhead after you go through Marble, which is famous for the Yule Marble Quarry. As you travel south on Colorado 133 toward the town of Marble look at the banks of the Crystal River and you will see large chunks of marble that fell off the train or were discarded. The marble from the Yule Quarry was used in the construction of several of America's national monuments, including the Tomb of the Unknown Soldier and the Lincoln Memorial. The quarry is in operation again after it was shut down for 63 years.

Once through Marble, on FR 314, you will be at the intersection with Forest Road 315. FR 315 is a 4-wheel-drive road, and taking it to the left leads to the trailhead. FR 314 (CR 3) goes straight to the abandoned Crystal Mill. This is a great place to get a photo of the old mill, because the Crystal River flows in front of it. Continuing straight on FR 314 will take you to the other end of FR 315. From this side, southeast on FR 314, it is a more difficult 4-wheel-drive road into Lead King Basin and the trailhead to Geneva Lake. Continuing straight on FR 314 will take you on a treacherous road over Schofield Pass to Crested Butte. The latter two roads are recommended only for highly skilled 4-wheel-drive enthusiasts.

13,620-foot Snowmass Peak on the left, 13,841-foot Hagerman Peak on the right, and 14,092-foot Snowmass Mountain peeking over the shoulder of Hagerman.

PHOTO BY ROD MARTINEZ

Traveling on FR 315 to Geneva Lake you will pass the Avalanche-Silver Creek Trail, which eventually leads to Avalanche Lake. Lead King Basin and the surrounding mountain valleys are filled with numerous varieties of wildflowers. At their peak in late spring and early summer they are head high in places and the colors are a blaze of rainbow hues. This is an incredible area to visit just for the wildflowers and the views of the mountain peaks that surround the basin on the eastern and southern edges, including Snowmass Mountain (14,092 feet), Hagerman Peak (13,841 feet), and Snowmass Peak (13,620 feet). Geneva Lake Trail continues for another 2.0 miles to 12,420-foot Trail Rider Pass, where the view of Snowmass Lake below is worth the hike. The views into Fravert Basin and of the highest peaks in the Maroon Bells-Snowmass Wilderness Area are amazing.

GETTING THERE: From the roundabout in Aspen travel 32 miles west on Colorado 82, then turn left at the intersection with CO 133. Travel south on CO 133 for 22.9 miles, turn left onto County Road 3 (also known as Forest Road 314), and go 6.0 miles through Marble, past Beaver Lake, for another 1.5 miles, until you reach the intersection with Forest Road

Lead King Basin Road cuts its way through meadows of wildflowers.

PHOTO BY ROD MARTINEZ

315, where you turn left on this 4-wheel-drive road. The trailhead is 6.5 miles from the intersection.

THE ROUTE: Although the sign indicating the Geneva Lake Trail is hard to find (tall wildflowers obscure it late in the season), the trail is easy to locate once you have descended the Lead King Basin Road (FR 315) to the heart of the basin. From the trailhead, the trail stays relatively level as it winds through a field of wildflowers for the first 0.1 mile, then a grove of aspens for 0.4 mile. Shortly after passing through the grove of aspens the trail intersects with the North Fork Fravert Basin Trail, which goes to the right. You are now in the Maroon Bells-Snowmass Wilderness Area. Here the trail begins to ascend and switchback up a steep slope, which is just to the left of a beautiful set of waterfalls. Almost all of the 1,200-foot elevation gain is attained during the next mile. About 1.5 miles from the trailhead the trail levels off

for the final 0.5 mile to Geneva Lake. There are a number of nice camping spots around the lake, and there are a few trees and an abundance of green grass and superb wildflowers in mid-summer. Retrace your steps back to the trailhead.

Waterfalls tumble out of Geneva Lake to provide water to wildflowers.

PHOTO BY ROD MARTINEZ

0 .1 .2 .3 .4 .5 .6 .7 .8 .9 1
MILES

9. Grizzly Lake Trail

BY ROD MARTINEZ

MAPS	Trails Illustrated, Aspen/Independence Pass, Number 127; USGS, Independence Pass 7.5 minute
ELEVATION GAIN	1,900 feet
RATING	Moderate
ROUND-TRIP DISTANCE	7.2 miles
ROUND-TRIP TIME	5–6 hours
NEAREST LANDMARK	Independence Pass

COMMENT: This hike reaches its high point in elevation and beauty when you cross over the final ridge and Grizzly Lake is revealed slightly below you. Reaching Grizzly Lake, at 12,550 feet, is only surpassed in beauty by the awe-inspiring 13,988-foot Grizzly Peak. You can get to Grizzly Lake via Independence Pass (Colorado 82) to Lincoln Road. At 12,095 feet, Independence Pass is typically closed seven months during a normal year and the area surrounding the pass will usually be covered in layers of snow and ice for six months of the year. As you hike farther into the backcountry to Grizzly Lake and other hikes, such as New York Creek (pages 78–81), keep in mind that there may be a considerable amount of snow on the trail in late spring or early summer. July through mid- to late September is the best time to hike the trails near Independence Pass.

In late spring and early summer you will be rewarded with beautiful meadows of wildflowers. In early fall you will be dazzled with the golden colors of the changing aspens. Take the time to visit the top of the pass, where this part of the Continental Divide separates the waters destined for the Pacific and Atlantic oceans. On a clear day

Early morning clouds over mountains to the northwest.

you can see all the way to the 14,110-foot Pikes Peak to the east and to the 14,150-foot Mount Sneffels to the southwest. Directly to the east are the two highest peaks in Colorado, 14,433-foot Mount Elbert and 14,421-foot Mount Massive.

GETTING THERE: From the ranger station in downtown Aspen, at the corner of West Hallam Street and North 7th Street, travel 10 miles to the east on CO 82 until you reach Lincoln Creek Road. Take a right here and at 0.5 mile keep left at the entrance to Lincoln Gulch Campground. After 6.3 miles—Grizzly Reservoir will be on your right—take a left and go about 0.1 mile. Just before you cross Grizzly Creek you will see a sign pointing to the trailhead on your left. If the parking spaces are occupied, cross the creek and park in the small parking area by the lake. Lincoln Creek Road does not require a 4-wheel-drive vehicle, but a high clearance vehicle is a must to clear some rocks, mounds, and mud holes.

THE ROUTE: The first 0.5 mile is steep as the trail switchbacks its way up and out of the coniferous forest to the beginning of a wide valley that leads you to Grizzly Peak. For the next 1.5 miles you will be on a fairly level trail as it winds

Grizzly Lake in all of its splendor at the base of 13,988-foot Grizzly Peak.

PHOTO BY ROD MARTINEZ

through stands of blue spruce. You will hike below some interesting outcroppings. After you have traveled 1.0 mile from the trailhead, you will cross a deep stream bed. At this point, you will notice that the trail wants to stay low; keep to the left on the higher and better maintained trail. You will go through a final grove of conifer trees and see the remains of an old cabin slightly upslope on your left. At 1.5 miles the trail will drop slightly and you will cross Grizzly Creek. After leaving the creek and a beautiful meadow of wildflowers, you will get your first view of the impressive north face of Grizzly Peak. For the next 2.0 miles the trail becomes steeper and narrower as you ascend the grassy slopes. At 3.2 miles from the trailhead, you will take a sharp left and begin your final ascent to the crest above Grizzly Lake. Hike over tundra for a few hundred feet to the northeastern end of the lake for a great spot to have lunch and savor Grizzly Peak looming above you. Retrace your steps back to the trailhead.

One of many meadows of wildflowers beside the trail to Grizzly Creek.

PHOTO BY ROD MARTINEZ

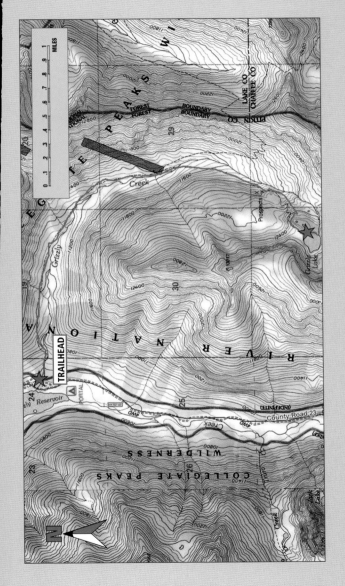

10. Hanging Lake Trail

BY ROD MARTINEZ

MAPS	Trails Illustrated, Flat Tops SE, Glenwood Canyon, Number 123; USGS, Storm King Mountain 7.5 minute
ELEVATION GAIN	1,150 feet
RATING	Difficult
ROUND-TRIP DISTANCE	3.2 miles
ROUND-TRIP TIME	2.5–3 hours
NEAREST LANDMARK	Glenwood Springs

COMMENT: Hanging Lake is one of nature's marvels. It is located in Glenwood Canyon, which is also home to one of man's marvels, Interstate 70. The natural wonders and engineering feats in Glenwood Canyon are nothing short of spectacular. The Colorado River carved the rugged and scenic Glenwood Canyon in west central Colorado as it cut down through the sedimentary rock. Four rest stops give you the opportunity to get out of your car and enjoy the Colorado River as well as the canyon walls that are 1,300 feet high in places. The most popular rest stop is Hanging Lake, which means if you want a parking space you need to arrive early, especially if you do this hike on the weekend.

Hanging Lake is the gem of Glenwood Canyon for a number of reasons, including the colored hues of green, blue, and aquamarine seen in the crystal clear water. The limestone cliffs and continual flow of water from Bridal Veil Falls have resulted in a lake hanging on a cliff. The lake's fragile shore, built up from carbonate deposits, requires visitors to stay on the Boy Scout-built boardwalk that rings the south shore. Because of its uniqueness and rare beauty, Hanging Lake was designated a National Natural Landmark in 2011.

Dead Horse Creek falls into Hanging Lake. PHOTO BY ROD MARTINEZ

GETTING THERE: From the roundabout in Aspen, follow Colorado 82 north for 42 miles to Glenwood Springs, where it intersects with I-70 eastbound. Take I-70 east for 9 miles to the Hanging Lake exit, #125.

THE ROUTE: The first 0.25 mile from the parking area is a walk, as you traverse a portion of the bike path that runs the length of Glenwood Canyon. After a bend in the path you will turn left at the drainage of Dead Horse Creek. The trail begins its ascent through a steep talus slope. Even though the trail is rocky in most places you should have sound footing thanks to frequent maintenance by the US Forest Service and the Boy Scouts. In the roughest places, and they are numerous, steps are carved into the rocks.

The trail intersects with the Dead Horse Trail in 0.25 mile, 0.5 mile from the trailhead. Stay on the main trail. As you continue to ascend and wind your way up the trail, you will cross the creek five or six times on well-maintained and sturdy wooden bridges. Take the time to enjoy the numerous waterfalls of Dead Horse Creek on your way up to Hanging Lake. Benches are placed along the trail; you

One of many waterfalls tumbling down from Hanging Lake to the Colorado River.

PHOTO BY ROD MARTINEZ

may need them to stop and catch your breath after some of the steeper spots along the trail.

After 1.3 miles, the trail will widen slightly and you will make a sharp turn to the right as you begin to follow the canyon wall on your left. A handrail on your right will assist with the steepness and large steps that are carved into the rock. Even though you will climb only 45 vertical feet, the hand rail is of great assistance in completing the steepest portion of the hike. You are now at the boardwalk. Follow it to the right for a few yards and you will see why Hanging Lake is a National

Natural Landmark. Continue to the end of the boardwalk as you enjoy Bridal Veil Falls across the lake. As you retrace your steps to the trailhead you may want to look for a sign at the steep portion that directs you to a short (about 100 feet) but steep trail to Spouting Rock, a waterfall spouting directly out of the face of a cliff.

Rockfalls in Glenwood Canyon, alongside the trail.

PHOTO BY ROD MARTINEZ

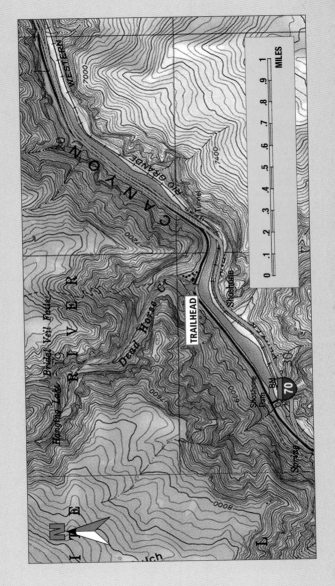

11. Maroon Bells Scenic Loop

BY ROD MARTINEZ

MAPS	Trails Illustrated, Maroon Bells/ Redstone/Marble, Number 128; USGS, Maroon Bells 7.5 minute
ELEVATION GAIN	Minimal to 100 feet
RATING	Easy
ROUND-TRIP DISTANCE	1.5 miles, which includes 0.5-mile loop around upper large pond
ROUND-TRIP TIME	1–1.5 hours
NEAREST LANDMARK	Maroon Lake

COMMENT: The epitome of beautiful landscapes is Maroon Lake reflecting the Maroon Bells. The Bells were given their name because of the maroon color and bell shape of the mountains. This is probably one of the most photographed scenes in all of North America. Because of this it is also one of the most visited areas in Colorado, so don't expect to be alone if you arrive here after 7 AM. The directions listed below are if you drive in using your own vehicle. The road is closed to vehicle traffic and you must take a shuttle bus from Aspen Highlands ski area to Maroon Lake after 9 AM, from June 15 through Labor Day or weekends during the fall. If you have questions regarding the bus service (normally only available when the road is closed to vehicle traffic), please call RFTA (Roaring Fork Transit Authority) at 970-925-8484. From 5 PM–9 AM the road is open to vehicles with a $10 recreation use fee, obtained at the ranger station. If you have a National Parks pass WITH a Golden Eagle Sticker, or a Golden Age/Access, or an America the Beautiful Pass you will not need to pay the fee. It is frustrating to drive most of the way to Maroon Lake only to be turned around at the ranger station because it is after 9 AM. Arriving early in the morning normally gives you a little peace and solitude, plus

The Maroon Bells reflected in Maroon Lake. PHOTO BY ROD MARTINEZ

the opportunity to photograph the Maroon Bells' reflection while the lake is still. You also increase your opportunity to see wildlife, especially deer and potentially moose. Maroon Lake, at 9,580 feet, is at the base of the Maroon Bells, which are two of the more infamous Fourteeners in Colorado. A US Forest Service sign on the access trail refers to these mountains as "The Deadly Bells" and warns would-be climbers of "down sloping, loose, rotten and unstable" rock that "kills without warning." The Bells got their "deadly" name in 1965 when eight people died in five separate accidents.

GETTING THERE: From downtown Aspen travel 0.5 mile to the roundabout and take a right on Maroon Creek Road. At 3.5 miles you will pass through the T-Lazy-7 Ranch before arriving at the ranger station at 5.0 miles. At 9.5 miles the road ends at the day-use parking lot and restroom facilities.

THE ROUTE: The trail begins at the west end of the parking lot just past the restrooms. For 0.5 mile follow the easy and wide path along the north side and to the end of Maroon Lake. In

Maroon Creek cascades from "The Bells" to Maroon Lake.

front of you the breathtaking panorama of the Maroon Bells unfolds. Stop, catch your breath, and take some photos. At the end of the lake you will see the large sign with information about the "Deadly Bells." At this point you can either cross the bridge or follow the narrow trail on the right, just a short distance before the bridge, to hike the upper portion of the scenic loop. After taking a right on the narrow trail, you will hike through an aspen forest as Maroon Creek accompanies you on your left. Shortly you will arrive at another bridge. The trail does not completely encircle Maroon Lake, so if you are short on time cross the bridge and walk back down to the parking lot. To do the upper part of the scenic loop, continue along the trail up and beyond the bridge. You'll continue on through the aspen forest for about 0.25 mile, and at times, will lose sight of the Maroon Bells. Keep working your way up; at some point you'll notice that you're walking back down

the mountain as you circle the upper small lake (pond). The waterfalls and cascades all along the banks of Maroon Creek add excitement to the tranquility of your hike. Continue back down the trail to the trailhead, once again enjoying the reflections and tranquility of Maroon Lake.

A red columbine.

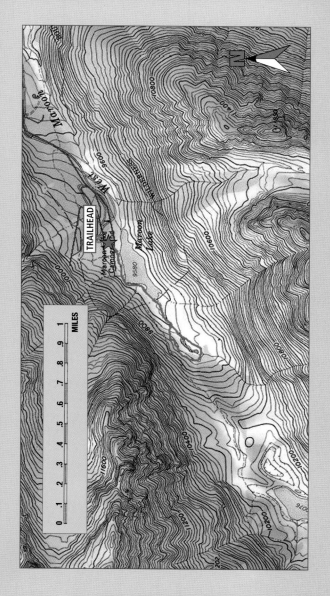

12. Midway Pass Trail

BY ROD MARTINEZ

MAPS	Trails Illustrated, Aspen/ Independence Pass, Number 127; USGS, Thimble Rock, Mount Champion, and Independence Pass 7.5 minute
ELEVATION GAIN	1,600 feet
RATING	Moderate–difficult
ROUND-TRIP DISTANCE	8.0 miles
ROUND-TRIP TIME	4–5 hours
NEAREST LANDMARK	Independence Pass

COMMENT: Midway Pass is another great hike east of Aspen on Independence Pass. This trail shares a trailhead with Lost Man Loop, which takes you to potentially four lakes on a 12.8-mile loop hike. As you're hiking the trail to Midway Pass, take some time to think about how the Ute Indians were able to flourish in this region, which was known for its biodiversity—from the riparian areas lower in the valley to the tundra of the higher mountains.

As you reach the high point of the trail above timberline you will pass by a number of tarns, along with rolling, grassy slopes filled with wildflowers that last late into the summer. The trail also offers superb views of a number of Fourteeners and Thirteeners, including 13,988-foot Grizzly Peak, in the wilderness areas south and west of Midway Pass. A large portion of the trail is located in the 82,026-acre Hunter-Fryingpan Wilderness Area, which is sandwiched between the wilderness areas of Holy Cross on the north, Maroon Bells-Snowmass on the west, and Collegiate Peaks on the south. My hikes on this trail have resulted in meeting very few hikers. Enjoy the beauty and the solitude.

A small lake near Midway Pass; it's a great place to rest before heading back.
PHOTO BY ROD MARTINEZ

GETTING THERE: From Aspen, travel 14.5 miles east on Colorado 82 to a large parking lot directly on the left, across from the Lost Man Campground.

THE ROUTE: In 0.5 mile from the trailhead at a large clearing there is an intersection with the Lost Man Trail on the right. Stay left and begin your ascent of Midway Trail and its 18 switchbacks. Some of the switchbacks are lengthy and others are rather short. Some make modest gains while others are long stretches of fairly steep ascent. The trail is well maintained and rocky in stretches, but it is easy to follow and hike if you take the time to catch your breath occasionally. All but about 400 of the 1,600 feet in elevation gain in this hike are in the 1.1 miles to the top of the switchbacks.

As you ascend through the forest the view through the trees opens so that the Thirteeners on your left are visible. Between the fourth and fifth switchbacks, about 0.75 mile from the trailhead, there is a nice rock outcropping on your left. Stop and enjoy the views of the mountains to the southeast that lead to the top of Independence Pass. Between switchbacks 7 and 8 and 10 and 11 the trail takes long steep ascents as you near the 1.1-mile mark. The remaining switchbacks are relatively short but very steep and rocky as you pass by a rock

A beautiful panoramic view of Pyramid Peak, the Maroon Bells, and Snowmass Mountain.   PHOTO BY ROD MARTINEZ

wall, scree slopes, and the sign for the Hunter-Fryingpan Wilderness Area. The trail continues on a long final ascent to the top and a plateau at 1.8 miles from the trailhead, where you are treated to great views of the Fourteeners—Maroon and North Maroon peaks, Snowmass Mountain, and Castle and Pyramid peaks—that reside in the Maroon Bells-Snowmass Wilderness Area, directly to the west. For another 1.0 mile the trail heads west through a large wet meadow of scrub willows and wildflowers. There is a small tarn to your left at 2.3 miles and a much larger one at 2.8 miles. This is a great place to enjoy the views with the tarn in front of you and the peaks in the distance. This is also a great place to turn around. The trail continues northwest for another 1.0 mile, where it takes a dip in elevation to Midway Pass. Midway Lake is about 0.75 mile farther down the trail from there. Retrace your steps back to the trailhead.

Looking up the valley toward Independence Pass.

PHOTO BY ROD MARTINEZ

13. Mount Sopris

BY ROD MARTINEZ

MAPS	Trails Illustrated, Maroon Bells/Redstone/Marble, Number 128 and Carbondale/Basalt, Number 143; USGS, Mount Sopris and Basalt 7.5 minute
ELEVATION GAIN	4,800 feet
RATING	Difficult–strenuous
ROUND-TRIP DISTANCE	11.6 miles
ROUND-TRIP TIME	10–12 hours
NEAREST LANDMARK	Carbondale

COMMENT: Mount Sopris is not quite 13,000 feet high, so it is not one of those coveted Fourteeners that hikers thirst to conquer. Because this mountain stands alone between Carbondale and Aspen, its dual 12,953-foot summits dominate the landscape. The elevation gain of this hike is 4,800 feet and the distance is 5.8 miles from the trailhead to the first (east) summit. These two factors give Mount Sopris a difficult-to-strenuous rating. If done in a day it certainly qualifies as strenuous. The Mount Sopris Trail will take you to the east summit. Once the east summit is reached you can hike to the west summit, but there is an elevation loss of 300 feet and then regained to climb to the west summit and then lost and regained again when you return to the east summit. The one-way distance between both summits is an additional 0.7 mile. Mount Sopris sits on the north end of the Elk Mountains and is located in the 181,117-acre Maroon Bells-Snowmass Wilderness Area. In comparison to other Elk Mountain trails (steep, rocky, and hazardous), this could be classified as an easy hike, but its 4,800-foot elevation gain and 11.6-mile round-trip distance make this a difficult-to-strenuous hike, especially if done as a day hike.

First snow on twin summits of 12,953-foot Mount Sopris.

PHOTO BY ROD MARTINEZ

GETTING THERE: From the roundabout in Aspen, drive 32 miles west on Colorado 82. Turn left on CO 133, travel south 2.0 miles, and then turn left on Prince Creek Road, County Road #5. Continue south for 6.0 miles until the road intersects with CR #6 (CR #5 ends here). Turn right on Forest Road #311 (Dinkle Lake Road), where a sign points to Dinkle Lake. Drive for about 2.0 miles and park in the large fenced parking lot on your left before you reach Dinkle Lake, 0.25 mile away.

THE ROUTE: The trailhead is located across the road from the large fenced parking area. The trail starts out as an old jeep trail as it leads you through an aspen forest. In a little more than 1.0 mile you will pass through some large open meadows that are full of waist-high wildflowers in late spring and early summer. Here you will have a great view of Mount Sopris; other views will come and go as you hike through a coniferous forest. At times the trail is rocky and steep as you ascend to Thomas Lakes. In about 3.4 miles from the trailhead there is a nice pond on your right, and after another 0.25 mile you will pass Lower Thomas Lake. On your way to Upper Thomas Lake, about another 0.25 mile, you will pass 10 designated camping spots. A few yards past Upper Thomas Lake are camping spots 11 to 13;

A great view of Thomas Lakes.

PHOTO BY ROD MARTINEZ

this is where the trail begins to get steeper as you work your way up the switchbacks.

As you gain altitude you will have access to the ridge, which eventually takes you west to the east summit. In 0.75 mile from the last designated camping spots (11–13) you will reach the beginning of the ridge as the vegetation becomes thin. In less than 0.5 mile you will be at tree line, and in a few feet more you will pass by the last tree where the ridge becomes narrow. As you continue to gain altitude this part of the trail may bother hikers who are afraid of heights. For the last 1.0 mile of the hike the trail fades in and out and is marked primarily by cairns. As the terrain becomes steeper and rockier you may have to use your hands to ascend because of loose rock. Within 0.5 mile of the top, you will encounter the first false summit. As you climb another 200 feet and go around the backside of this first false summit you will see the second and final false summit. Several hundred feet away, but with only a 30-foot gain in elevation, the east summit is finally completed. Once on the top, the 360-degree views are wondrous and beautiful. The west summit of Mount Sopris is now directly in front of you. As you retrace your steps to the trailhead, remember that it is slow, tedious, and dangerous descending to Thomas Lakes because of the steep scree slopes.

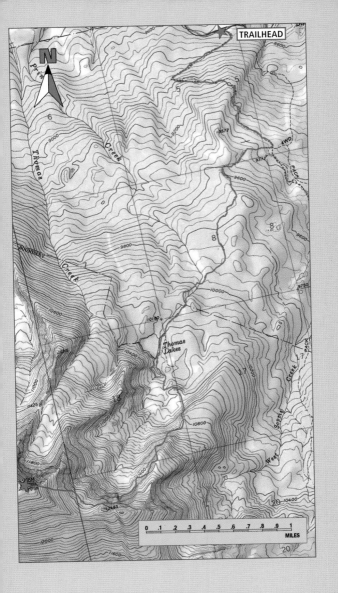

TRAILHEAD

14. Native Lake Trail

BY CHRISTIAN GREEN

MAPS	Trails Illustrated, Aspen/Independence Pass, Number 127; USGS, Mount Massive 7.5 minute
ELEVATION GAIN	2,100 feet
RATING	Moderate
ROUND-TRIP DISTANCE	7.8 miles
ROUND-TRIP TIME	5–6 hours
NEAREST LANDMARK	Leadville

COMMENT: In Colorado, the seasons can turn in the blink of an eye, so take that into account before attempting this high-elevation hike, which starts at 10,774 feet and climbs to nearly 12,000 feet. The Native Lake Trail is best hiked between July and mid-September. By the second weekend of October, when I hiked this trail, snow had already fallen heavily (about a foot) in this section of the San Isabel National Forest, just west of Leadville. Although the newly fallen snow made for a pristine landscape, it also made the hike more difficult. Furthermore, the middle portion—a little past the 2.0-mile mark—of this hike is around tree line, so 30-to-40-plus mph winds and/or lightning may also come into play when hiking this trail. That said, from the trail's highpoint, the panorama of Colorado's second-highest peak, Mount Massive (14,421 feet), and other northern Sawatch peaks, is impressive, as are the views of the many lakes that dot the landscape below. **Note:** Native Lake Trail is the same trail as Highline Trail, except the latter continues past Native Lake to the Leadville National Fish Hatchery, 9.4 miles from the trailhead.

GETTING THERE: During the summer, when Independence Pass is open, take CO 82 east over the pass to US 24 (just

Native Lake from above, on a snowy early October day.

PHOTO BY CHRISTIAN GREEN

under 40 miles). Make a left and head north on US 24 for approximately 14.0 miles to mile marker 177, which is just south of downtown Leadville. There you will make a left on McWethy Drive/County Road 4. Continue on CR 4 for a little more than 4.0 miles, until you reach Sugarloaf Dam, at the southeastern tip of Turquoise Lake. At this point, CR 4 becomes Turquoise Lake Road. Follow CR 4/Turquoise Lake Road for approximately 3.3 miles, as it parallels the southern shore of Turquoise Lake, until the road forks. Take the left fork away (southwest) from the lake. CR 4 now turns into Forest Road 105/Hagerman Pass Road, which you will follow for just over 3.5 miles. Although this road is not paved, most 2-wheel drive cars can make it to the trailhead parking lot, which is on the left, or south side, of the road.

If Independence Pass is closed due to snow (typically from November 1 through Memorial Day), travel north on CO 82 from Aspen to I-70, which you will take east toward Denver. Take exit 171 (CO 24) and head south (just over 30 miles) to Leadville. In Leadville, make a right onto 6th Avenue and follow it until it runs into McWethy Drive (less than 1.0 mile). Make a right onto McWethy Drive and follow the directions above.

THE ROUTE: The trailhead is on the south side of the parking area, which has room for several cars. At the trailhead, you can take a quick look at the wooden placards, which include a trail map and information on Colorado's state fish, the greenback cutthroat trout. Once you pass the informational signs, the trail heads into a fir/spruce forest and past a couple of small streams. After 0.25 mile or so from the trailhead, the trail begins to open up and turns toward the east, paralleling Hagerman Pass Road. Here, the trail becomes a bit steeper and there are sections with a bit of exposure on the left, or north, side. This area can be particularly precarious if there's snow on the trail, so proceed with care. After about 0.5 mile, the trail begins to level out again and then switchbacks up the ridge. As you make your way back and forth up the ridge, the trail crosses an unnamed tributary of Busk Creek a few times.

After approximately 2.0 miles, you approach tree line and a large expanse of tundra, dotted by small tarns and diminutive coniferous trees. This part of the trail is marked by a set of wooden poles, which are very helpful in guiding the hiker when the trail is covered in snow. The views from this segment of the hike are breathtaking, with Mount Massive and the Centennial Mount Oklahoma (13,845 feet) looming just a few miles to the south. Several lakes, including Swamp Lakes, dot the landscape to the east. On a clear day, Leadville and the Arkansas Valley can also be seen to the east/southeast. Once you cross the tundra (around 0.5 mile), the trail switchbacks about 1.0 mile down to Native Lake, approximately 500 feet (in elevation) below. As you make your way down to just west of the lake, keep an eye out for a short spur trail that takes you the final few hundred feet to Native Lake. Once there, you can grab some lunch on one of the many boulders on the other side of the lake, snap a few photos of one of central Colorado's most beautiful high alpine lakes, or even fish (catch and release only) for greenback cutthroat trout. Once you've had a chance to take in the grandeur of this alluring lake and basin, retrace your steps back to the trailhead.

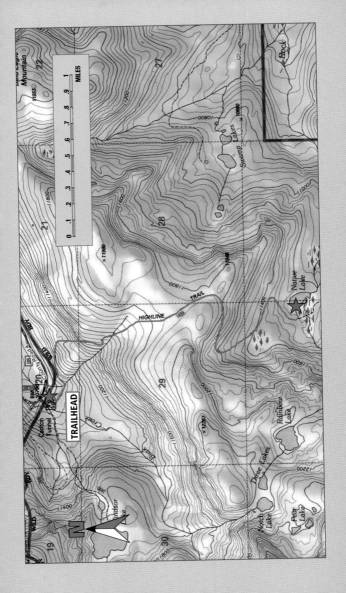

15. New York Creek Trail

BY ROD MARTINEZ

MAPS	Trails Illustrated, Aspen/Independence Pass, Number 127; USGS, New York Peak 7.5 minute
ELEVATION GAIN	2,160 feet
RATING	Moderate–difficult
ROUND-TRIP DISTANCE	8.4 miles
ROUND-TRIP TIME	5–6 hours
NEAREST LANDMARK	Independence Pass

COMMENT: New York Creek is one of the trails in the Lincoln Creek drainage. It winds its way up to an unnamed pass about 4.4 miles southwest of the trailhead. At the top of the pass the trail continues to the old town site of Ashcroft. Viewing the remnants of old cabins, waterwheels, and other mining artifacts of Ashcroft and other ghost towns located in the Independence Pass and Aspen areas pique your interest as to what routes the miners used to traverse the area passes on their way to the then thriving "cities" of Buena Vista or Leadville. Many of these old mining trails are now hiking trails, on which we can enjoy the picturesque views that the miners presumably witnessed during their everyday lives.

GETTING THERE: From the ranger station in downtown Aspen travel 10 miles to the east on Colorado 82 until you reach Lincoln Creek Road. Take a right here and at 0.5 mile keep left as you pass the entrance to Lincoln Gulch Campground on your right. At 3.1 miles, the New York Creek Trailhead and a small parking lot will be on your right. Lincoln Creek Road does not require a 4-wheel-drive vehicle, but a high clearance vehicle is a must to make it past some rocks, mounds, and mud holes.

New York Creek Pass lies straight ahead.

PHOTO BY ROD MARTINEZ

THE ROUTE: A few yards from the small parking area and trail-head you will have to cross (ford) Lincoln Creek. The creek may be tricky to ford during late spring and early summer because of the increased water flow from the runoff of melting snow. There are no bridges, logs, or rocks to help you cross the creek. Once you are on the other side, recon-nect with the trail. The trail begins to ascend gradually, but in about 0.1 mile the trail becomes steeper as it turns into an old jeep road and you enter an evergreen forest for the next 1.0 mile. You will then exit the evergreen forest into a clearing where you will hike steeply uphill for about 0.2 mile before the trail merges with an old aqueduct road. Make note of your entrance to this road, because you will have to locate it when you head back to the trailhead. There is a small sign here, but it is hard to spot.

At this point you will get a great look at 12,811-foot New York Peak. A little after 0.25 mile from the small sign, you will pass by the diversion dam for Brooklyn Gulch and its stream. Continue on the aqueduct road as it makes a big sweeping "s" curve and then straightens. In about 5 minutes you will see the New York Creek diversion dam. A few yards before the diversion you will see a sign and a trail

Williams Mountain Range to the south of the pass.

PHOTO BY ROD MARTINEZ

on your left; turn left here for the continuation of the New York Creek Trail. Reenter the woods and ascend through the spruce forest as you listen to and catch glimpses of New York Creek as it descends to Lincoln Creek. After about 1.0 mile of steep climbs through the forest and meadows, the trail crosses a small secondary stream. The trail continues steeply for another 0.25 mile, at which point you will reach a section of large and beautiful meadows. The trail begins to fade, but you are guided by posts and cairns as you move through marshy or snow-covered tundra to the pass about 0.25 mile ahead. Take the time to sit down and enjoy the 360-degree panoramic view. Retrace your steps back to the inevitable ford of Lincoln Creek at the trailhead.

12,811-foot New York Peak.

PHOTO BY ROD MARTINEZ

16. Rio Grande Trail

BY ROD MARTINEZ

MAPS	Trails Illustrated, Aspen/Independence Pass, Number 127; USGS, Independence Pass 7.5 minute
ELEVATION GAIN	Minimal
RATING	Easy
ROUND-TRIP DISTANCE	4–5+ miles
ROUND-TRIP TIME	1.5–2 hours
NEAREST LANDMARK	Aspen

COMMENT: Aspen has many trails that begin in the city, some of which branch out from the 42-mile Rio Grande Trail that makes its way to Glenwood Springs. Besides the Rio Grande Trail, other Aspen trails are Hunter Creek, 6.5 miles one way; Smuggler Mountain Trail, 1.5 miles one way; Sunnyside Trail, 6.3 miles one way; Ute Trail, 1.1 miles one way (described on pages 94–97 of this pack guide); and East of Aspen Trail, 3.1+ miles one way. Some of these trails are easy, others are moderate and/or difficult, but the Rio Grande Trail is paved the first 2.0 miles and is wheelchair accessible. The most difficult part of this trail is finding parking, because it is limited and normally only for two hours.

The Rio Grande Trail is part of the old Denver and Rio Grande Railroad Aspen Branch rail corridor. At different times from the 1960s to the mid-1990s train operations ended in phases. Great Outdoors Colorado, the Colorado Department of Transportation, Pitkin County Open Space and Trails, and local governments purchased the rail corridor and tracks to explore transportation alternatives to address congestion on Colorado 82 and create recreation connectivity in the Roaring Fork Valley that extends

Roaring Fork River, along Rio Grande Trail.   PHOTO BY ROD MARTINEZ

from Aspen to Glenwood Springs, 42 miles to the north. The Roaring Fork Transportation Authority manages and maintains the Rio Grande Trail, along with other partner agencies in the Roaring Fork Valley.

For the first 2.0 miles the trail is 8 to 10 feet wide hard surfaced (paved with some concrete sections) with soft shoulders that are 2 to 6 feet wide. The remaining 40 miles to Glenwood have more asphalt and concrete sections interspersed with hard-packed gravel. The paved segment is very popular with walkers, joggers, runners, and cyclists and a great hike for visitors to adjust to the altitude. The trail parallels the Roaring Fork River, crosses Hunter Creek near the Aspen post office, and gives you access to other local trails. Because of the many cyclists, keep these dos and don'ts in mind: Walk on the right coming and going; be aware of bikers, who should pass you on the left and warn you that they are passing using a bell or calling out "on the left"; enjoy wildlife at a distance—approaching wildlife or harassing wildlife is prohibited and could be dangerous; use a leash for your pet and pick up after it; respect and stay off adjacent private property; and respect the solitude by keeping your voice and music down, so that you and other hikers can enjoy the sounds of the wildlife and the Roaring Fork River.

There's more solitude along the trail, as you travel north from Aspen.

PHOTO BY ROD MARTINEZ

GETTING THERE: From Main Street in downtown Aspen turn north on Mill Street and go 0.2 mile to Puppy Smith Road. The entrance is to the north of the Aspen Post Office and slightly east of the Aspen Center for Environmental Studies and the John Denver Sanctuary.

THE ROUTE: After finding a parking spot, you will see the trail entrance slightly to the north. Within a few yards you will cross over the Roaring Fork River and then within 0.1 mile you will cross Hunter Creek on another bridge. For the duration of this hike the Roaring Fork River will follow you on your left. There are numerous benches along the trail, as well as numerous wildflowers. At 1.5 miles from the trailhead take a curve to the left where you will go under Cemetery Lane Road. Henry Stein Park is 2.2 miles into the hike and a great place to take a break or even fish. In this small park take a short dirt trail to see some Class IV rapids on the Roaring Fork River. At 2.4 miles the trail turns to compacted gravel and intersects with the Sunnyside Trail. As you retrace your steps back to the trailhead take the time to explore the Jenny Adair Wetlands next to Puppy Smith Road. The Jenny Adair Wetlands is an easy-to-access park where you can see local wetland species, such as swallows, warblers, dragonflies, damselflies, Lewis monkeyflower, Rocky Mountain iris, small-winged sedge, American three-square bulrush, narrowleaf cottonwood, thin-leaf alder, bog birch, and Redosier dogwood.

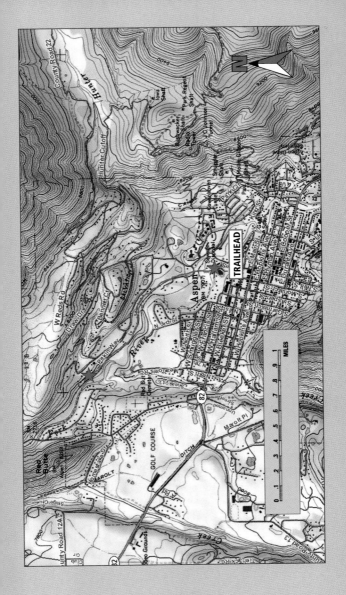

17. Storm King Mountain Memorial Trail

BY ROD MARTINEZ

MAPS	Trails Illustrated Flat Tops SE, Glenwood Canyon, Number 123; USGS, Shoshone 7.5 minute
ELEVATION GAIN	1,000 feet
RATING	Difficult
ROUND-TRIP DISTANCE	3.0 miles to observation point; 4.0 miles to memorial sites
ROUND-TRIP TIME	2–3 hours
NEAREST LANDMARK	Interstate 70

COMMENT: Storm King Mountain is not your average hike, because the trail ascends more than 700 feet in a mile and then drops about 170 feet into a ravine before it climbs another 500 feet in 0.5 mile. This trail is difficult and not for the fainthearted in a couple of different ways. The trail was built by volunteers as a memorial to 14 firefighters—both men and women, none of whom were from Colorado—who lost their lives on July 6, 1994. The firefighters came to battle a seemingly benign blaze, officially named the South Canyon Fire, near Glenwood Springs, that was started by a single bolt of lightning, smoldered for days, and then was fanned by wind. As you hike the trail remember that sadly it only exists for 14 reasons: Kathi Beck, Tami Bickett, Scott Blecha, Levi Brinkley, Robert Browning Jr., Doug Dunbar, Terri Hagen, Bonnie Holtby, Rob Johnson, Jon Kelso, Don Mackey, Roger Roth, Jim Thrash, and Richard Tyler. At the trailhead, hikers find several signs explaining what went wrong on July 6, 1994, and the stories of the people who lost their lives that day. This trail is not meant to be easy; it is difficult, it can be strenuous, and it gives you a sense of the terrain the firefighters had to deal with on that day. This is

Memorial signs at trailhead.

how and where the 14 firefighters went to extinguish the beginnings of the fire.

GETTING THERE: From the roundabout in Aspen travel 42 miles north on CO 82 to Glenwood Springs. Take I-70 west, approximately 5 miles, to exit #109, Canyon Creek. Take a quick right onto the frontage road, where a small sign will point you to the parking lot for the trailhead, 0.9 mile east.

THE ROUTE: The trail begins steep and rough, which is very similar to what the firefighters encountered, except they had no trail to follow. As you wind your way through junipers to the top of the hill (about 1.0 mile) you will see I-70 and the Colorado River below you. As you continue the ascent the hustle and bustle and noise of I-70 does not go away, it remains a constant reminder that life goes on. The first 1.0 mile of this hike is well maintained but gains 700 feet in elevation and is the most difficult portion of the first part of the trail. On your way to the top you will pass occasional signs that describe information about wildfires, as well as one that explains what the area looked like before the fire. At the top of the hill the trail levels off and in another 0.5 mile you will be at the observation point. Here you will see the place across the valley where the firefighters were building a fire line. You can stop here and retrace your steps back to the trailhead or you can continue on the trail as it drops 170 feet into a ravine in the valley before it begins a 500-foot almost vertical climb in the next 0.5 mile.

Trail from observation point memorializing spots where firefighters died.

PHOTO BY ROD MARTINEZ

During the 500-foot climb, the trail is very rugged and steep; stairs were added to assist visitors make the climb to the memorials. At the top of the rise the trail splits; turn right to see trees covered in T-shirts and other mementos left behind by other firefighters to pay tribute to their fallen colleagues. A short steep trail takes you to another observation point and the lower trail takes you to the spots, marked by crosses, where the 12 smokejumpers were killed. When you return to the main trail, there is another 0.3-mile side trail to the right that takes you to another site where two more firefighters were working at a helispot (landing area for helicopters). Memorials denote the site where these two firefighters also lost their lives. As you retrace your steps to the trailhead remember the 14 firefighters who lost their lives on Storm King Mountain. This trail takes you on a journey through burned land that is now recovering, and provides the hiker insight to the feelings and work of all of those who fight wildland fires.

Looking west along I-70 and the Colorado River as you hike up the trail.

PHOTO BY ROD MARTINEZ

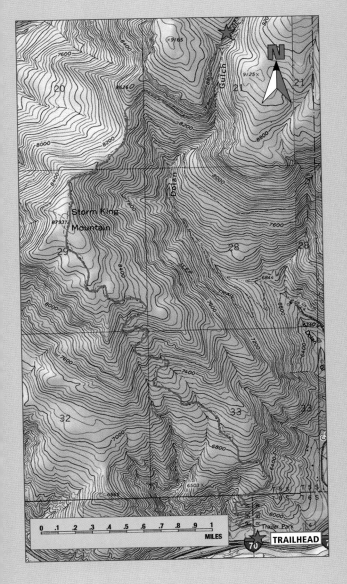

18. Timberline Lake Trail

BY CHRISTIAN GREEN

MAPS	Trails Illustrated, Holy Cross/ Reudi Reservoir, Number 126; USGS, Homestake Reservoir 7.5 minute
ELEVATION GAIN	855 feet
RATING	Easy
ROUND-TRIP DISTANCE	4.4 miles (more if you continue hiking along the western side of the lake)
ROUND-TRIP TIME	3–4 hours (plus time to enjoy the lake)
NEAREST LANDMARK	Leadville

COMMENT: If you're looking for an easy hike near Leadville, Timberline Lake Trail is an excellent choice. A relatively level and short trail leads to a remarkably beautiful lake, which not only offers picturesque views of the lake's placid waters, but also of the surrounding Holy Cross Wilderness Area. The lake also offers some good catch-and-release fishing for Colorado's state fish, the greenback cutthroat trout, which was reintroduced into the lake by the Division of Wildlife in the spring of 1999. During wet summers, the trail is also a prime location to spot wild mushrooms, such as the poisonous Amanita muscaria (a red-capped mushroom, with white or yellow warts), which grows in close proximity to the many coniferous trees that line the trail.

GETTING THERE: During the summer, when Independence Pass is open, take CO 82 east from Aspen over the pass to US 24 (just under 40 miles). Make a left and head north on US 24 for approximately 14.0 miles to mile marker 177, which is just south of downtown Leadville. There you will make a left on McWethy Drive/County Road 4. Continue on CR 4 for 1.5

Timberline Lake, from the end of the trail.   PHOTO BY CHRISTIAN GREEN

miles, then turn right onto CR 9, which you will follow for 1.5 miles. Turn left (staying on CR 9) across from the large parking area (Leadville Junction) and cross the railroad tracks and Tennessee Creek. At the T-intersection (less than 0.5 mile from Leadville Junction), take a right (north) onto Turquoise Lake Road (also CR 9) and drive 7.0 miles (Turquoise Lake will be on your left for a good portion of this section of the road) to 104E, which is a short dirt road (less than 0.1 mile) that takes you to a small parking area for both Timberline Lake and segments 9 and 10 of The Colorado Trail.

If Independence Pass is closed, travel north on CO 82 from Aspen to I-70, where you will head east toward Denver. Take exit 171 (CO 24) and head south (just over 30 miles) to Leadville. In Leadville, make a right onto 6th Avenue and follow it until it runs into McWethy Drive (less than 1.0 mile). Make a right onto McWethy Drive and follow the directions above.

THE ROUTE: The trailhead is on the northwestern side of the small parking area, and both the Continental Divide and The Colorado Trails can be accessed from here. Shortly after starting the hike (less than 0.1 mile), you will cross a bridge that takes you over Lake Fork, a stream that flows out of Turquoise Lake. You will actually be on The Colorado Trail for about 0.25 mile when you come to a split in the trail. At this juncture, The Colorado Trail heads off to the left (south), while Timberline Lake Trail, which is marked by two large metal Xs (in the ground), heads west toward the lake. Within a few hundred feet of the split, you will see a sign for the Holy Cross Wilderness Area, which you are about to enter.

The first two-thirds of the trail is fairly level, going in and out of stands of evergreens. In the shady, wooded areas, many varieties of mushrooms can be spotted near the trail. However, be aware that some of these mushrooms are poisonous and should not be eaten. While heading up to Timberline Lake, you will also pass through several small meadows, many of which contain wildflowers during mid-summer. For the length of the trail, Lake Fork flows just off to the right and then the left, and a couple of times it crosses the trail; it can easily be forded during the summer and fall, via rock footpaths in the creek.

At about 1.5 miles into the hike, the trail begins to ascend toward the lake, as you gain a few hundred feet in elevation. This is the only portion of the hike that gets the heart pumping. However, the trail quickly levels out again after only about 0.25 mile. Once you reach the lake, at approximately 2.2 miles, grab your camera and take a minute to savor the pristine views of the lake. You can then continue for a few tenths of a mile along the southern and western end of the lake, which takes you to a marshy area where a small stream enters Timberline Lake, on the north side. Be aware that the trail ends before you get to Lake Fork, although there are a couple of social trails on the east side of the lake.

Timberline Lake Trail is a great hike for families, but it can often get crowded during summer weekends. It's also a nice spot for a picnic and for trying your luck at catching greenback cutthroat trout. Once you spend some time admiring the beauty of Timberline Lake and enjoying some lunch, retrace your steps and head back down the path toward the parking area.

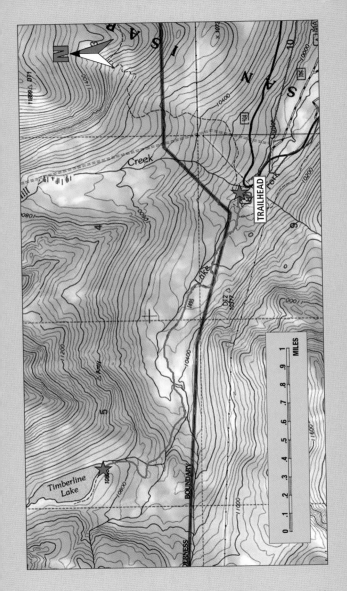

19. Ute Trail

BY ROD MARTINEZ

MAPS	Trails Illustrated, Aspen/ Independence Pass, Number 127; USGS, Independence Pass 7.5 minute
ELEVATION GAIN	1,200 feet
RATING	Difficult
ROUND-TRIP DISTANCE	2.2 miles
ROUND-TRIP TIME	1.5–2 hours
NEAREST LANDMARK	Aspen

COMMENT: John Denver's "Rocky Mountain High" aptly describes Aspen's ski trails, hundreds of miles of hiking trails, and the high peaks that are the monarchs of the Roaring Fork Valley. At the south end of town, Aspen Mountain towers over a place that is a destination for many visitors any time of the year. During the last few years, some of Aspen's more famous visitors have been black bears. Because of recent drought conditions in the Aspen area, along with the depletion of natural food sources, more black bears are entering the Aspen area to rummage through dumpsters, campers, tents, and other sources of food. Keep your food in bear tamper-proof containers, locked in a closed vehicle, or if carried while hiking, placed in airtight containers. Bears have appeared and will appear anywhere in the Aspen area, including along Ute Trail. If you encounter a bear, stay calm, avoid eye contact but continue to face the bear, walk away if possible, or stop and give the bear an escape route as you speak softly. If possible step off the trail on the downhill side and leave the area. If you come across a cub, walk away slowly and avoid getting between the cub and the mother. If a bear moves toward you do not run. Bears can run up to 35 mph and can easily

View of west Aspen from Ute Trail.   PHOTO BY ROD MARTINEZ

outrun any human uphill or downhill. Bears are also great tree climbers. By doing the above you should greatly lessen any attack by a bear, but if you are attacked fight back with rocks, sticks, your camera, and even your bare hands. Make lots of noise and make yourself look bigger (with arms extended and with your coat) if being attacked. It may be "neat" or "cool" to get a great picture or to feed a bear, but DO NOT DO THIS, leave them alone and they will probably leave you alone as well. Bears are looking for food, not to take a hike.

Ute Trail is a difficult trail. It gains 1,200 feet in elevation in little more than a mile. This trail will test your leg muscles and heart on the way up. It will give your knees a great workout on the way down. Most of the people I met on this trail were hiking rapidly up and down, or jogging or running up the trail. It is a great workout, and I am sure it keeps a lot of Aspenites in great shape for hiking or skiing.

GETTING THERE: Take Colorado 82 east about 0.4 mile to Original Street, turn right and follow Original Street about 0.6 mile to Ute Avenue, then turn left and go 0.4 mile to a small parking lot near the trailhead.

A perfect bird's-eye view.

PHOTO BY ROD MARTINEZ

THE ROUTE: This trail is not very long (1.1 miles one way) and certainly not hard to follow, but it is steep, rocky, and travels by some precarious slopes and drop-offs. The trail is located across from the small parking lot where a small sign can be found designating Ute Trail. For the first 0.33 mile you will steeply ascend through scrub oak and small aspens. The switchbacks lead you farther uphill into a forest of conifers and larger aspens. About 0.5 mile from the trailhead you will get a great view of the Aspen Club when you look down into Aspen. As you continue upwards, views across the valley begin to open. At 0.75 mile from the trailhead you will take a sharp turn to the right to begin your final steep ascent to your destination. This part of the trail is extremely rocky before it levels off for the last 0.1 mile to the large rock outcropping. Take a break and enjoy the views before you retrace your steps back down the steep, rocky trail to the trailhead.

20. West Maroon Trail

BY ROD MARTINEZ

MAPS	Trails Illustrated, Maroon Bells/ Redstone/Marble, Number 128; USGS, Maroon Bells 7.5 minute
ELEVATION GAIN	1,500 feet
RATING	Moderate–difficult
ROUND-TRIP DISTANCE	7.6 miles
ROUND-TRIP TIME	6–8 hours
NEAREST LANDMARK	Maroon Lake

COMMENT: Initially I was going to hike through the West Maroon Valley along the bases of the Fourteeners North Maroon (14,014 feet), Maroon (14,156 feet), and Pyramid (14,018 feet) peaks to West Maroon Pass. But the trail was much longer than anticipated, 13 miles round trip, with almost 3,000 feet in elevation gain, making this a difficult to strenuous day hike, rather than the desired moderate to difficult hike I planned on. The trail also crossed West Maroon Creek a few times and the water levels required equipment I did not have. If you continue past the turn-around point, the first major crossing of West Maroon Creek, I highly recommend water shoes of some sort. Some hikers that crossed the creek had sandals or lightweight tennis shoes that they wore to ford the stream. Those who did not had to stop on the other side and empty the water from their boots and change socks.

The hike to this point is incredibly beautiful as you traverse through a valley full of wildflowers in late spring and early summer. In fall the aspens along the base of the mountains are turning gold. As the trail approaches Crater Lake you will begin to see waterfalls on the western wall of mountains where they descend to West Maroon Creek. Be sure to turn around and look down the valley at West Maroon Creek as

The Bells and Sleeping Sexton from the shore of Crater Lake.

PHOTO BY ROD MARTINEZ

it snakes its way to Crater Lake then to Maroon Lake. The trail continues past North Maroon and Maroon peaks to the top of West Maroon Pass, where it then descends for 4.5 miles to the west trailhead 1.0 mile south of Schofield Pass. This makes for a great shuttle hike from Crested Butte back to Aspen. At the first major crossing of West Maroon Creek and at the base of some terrific waterfalls I turned around to avoid hiking in wet boots and socks.

GETTING THERE: From downtown Aspen travel 0.5 mile to the roundabout and take a right (west) on Maroon Creek Road. Arrive at the ranger station at 5.0 miles. At 9.5 miles the road ends at the very large day-use parking lot. Please read the vehicle restrictions and fees that are described in the Maroon Bells Scenic Loop on page 62 of this pack guide.

THE ROUTE: The trail begins at the west end of the parking lot. To the right of the US Forest Service bulletin board, 0.5 mile from the trailhead and at the end of Maroon Lake, look for a small sign for the trail to Crater Lake. For further description of the hike to Crater Lake, please read the trail route as described in this pack guide on pages 38–41. At 1.7 miles from the trailhead, you will emerge into a short grassy meadow at the edge of Crater Lake. The trail separates, with the right-hand branch going to Buckskin Pass. The main trail, on the left side, continues on for about 5.0 miles, via

Looking east to a frost-shrouded Crater Lake.

PHOTO BY ROD MARTINEZ

a long climb to the far end of the valley at 12,500-foot West Maroon Pass. For the last 0.33 mile, hike alongside Crater Lake until you reach the southern end of the lake where Pyramid Peak begins to reveal its beauty.

From here the trail follows a level grade through meadows of wildflowers, then a sea of willows, before entering the forest and climbing steeply through a rock slide at 2.8 miles from the trailhead. After this rockslide and at the base of Maroon Peak you will cross a large (100 to 150 feet across) avalanche or water chute that was formed in 2013. The trail levels and then descends to a stand of conifers at the base of another large rockslide after 3.2 miles from the trailhead. Cross a small creek and continue for about 0.5 mile as you cross another large open rockslide and pass a beautiful waterfall on your left. In another 0.1 mile you will come to the first major creek crossing. If you are prepared, ford West Maroon Creek and continue on. This is where the hike turns around; retrace your steps to the trailhead. **Note:** If you continue on to the crest of West Maroon Pass, it is another 2.7 miles one way, with an elevation gain of 1,500 feet, of which 800 feet is done in the last 0.7 mile. The view both ways is incredible, as you look either way to see emerald green meadows with a profusion of wildflowers. As you look back to the east from the top of the pass, you will have a great view of Pyramid Peak and the Maroon Bells. To the west your view extends to the Treasure Mountains.

THE BEST ASPEN HIKES

About the Author

Rod Martinez has always loved spending time outside. As a kid growing up in Cripple Creek, he explored the nearby hills and old mines. As he grew older, he found another love—photography. In time he discovered 35mm photography and a lifelong passion was born. Rod has climbed 17 of Colorado's Fourteeners and has hiked in almost all of the Western states, primarily in Colorado, Utah, and northern Arizona. He has been able to combine his two passions to visually capture nature's beauty on every hike. His work has resulted in him being named Grand Junction's Photographer of the Year for four years in a row. In 2001, he helped form the Southwest Photographic Arts Association Camera Club, and he currently teaches photography and leads photo workshops. Rod joined the Colorado Mountain Club in 2000 and has served as the program director for the Western Slope Group and currently acts as treasurer and trail steward for the group.

Colorado 82 continues its journey from east Aspen to Independence Pass.

PHOTO BY ROD MARTINEZ

Waterfalls from Thunder Pyramid cascading down to West Maroon Creek Trail turnaround point.

PHOTO BY ROD MARTINEZ

THE BEST ASPEN HIKES

Checklist

THE BEST ASPEN HIKES